Counseling
Multiracial
Families

MULTICULTURAL ASPECTS OF COUNSELING SERIES

SERIES EDITOR

Paul Pedersen, Ph.D., *University of Alabama at Birmingham*

EDITORIAL BOARD

VOLUMES IN THIS SERIES

Counseling Multiracial Families

Bea Wehrly
Kelley R. Kenney
Mark E. Kenney

Multicultural Aspects of Counseling Series 12

SAGE Publications
International Educational and Professional Publisher
Thousand Oaks   London   New Delhi

For information:

SAGE Publications, Inc.
2455 Teller Road
Thousand Oaks, California 91320
E-mail: order@sagepub.com

SAGE Publications Ltd.
6 Bonhill Street
London EC2A 4PU
United Kingdom

SAGE Publications India Pvt. Ltd.
M-32 Market
Greater Kailash I
New Delhi 110 048 India

Printed in the United States of America

Library of Congress Cataloging-in-Publication Data

Wehrly, Bea, 1926–
    Counseling multiracial families / by Bea Wehrly, Kelley R. Kenney,
Mark E. Kenney.
       p. cm.—(Multicultural aspects of counseling series; v. 12)
    Includes bibliographical references.
    ISBN 0-7619-1590-7 (cloth: alk. paper)
    ISBN 0-7619-1591-5 (pbk.: alk. paper)
    1. Family counseling. 2. Cross-cultural counseling. 3. Racially mixed
people—Counseling of. 4. Interracial marriage. 5. Interracial adoption.
I. Kenney, Kelley R. II. Kenney, Mark E. III. Title. IV. Series.
HV697 .W43 1999
362.84—dc21   99-6282

This book is printed on acid-free paper.

99 00 01 02 03 04 05 7 6 5 4 3 2 1

Acquiring Editor:	Kassie Gavrilis
Editorial Assistant:	Heidi Van Middlesworth
Production Editor:	Wendy Westgate
Editorial Assistant:	Patricia Zeman
Typesetter:	Lynn Miyata
Cover Designer:	Candice Harman
Indexer:	Molly Hall

Contents

Series Editor's Introduction

Our families have typically been the source of those culturally learned assumptions that control our lives, with or without our permission. For that reason it is especially important for us to include Wehrly, Kenney, and Kenney's excellent volume in the **Multicultural Aspects of Counseling** book series. All families are complicated, but some families are more complicated than others. This is particularly true when those families are multicultural and/or multiracial and when all the complications associated with multiculturalism have been treated as "problematic." These complications, however, offer opportunities as well as special problems, and Wehrly et al. go into some detail about those special opportunities in the historical and sociopolitical environments of our multicultural society.

When I was a faculty member at the University of Malaya during the race riots of 1969, the faculty members were recruited to continue teaching courses in the university dormitories so that the students would not become involved in the riots. In one of my classes, we decided to use creative problem solving techniques in small groups to "solve" the racial problem in Malaysia. The criterion was to identify solutions that had never been tried. The group that was identified as having the most creative solution suggested (a) that something be put into the drinking water changing everyone to the same color, whichever color that might be; (b) that kissing replace handshakes as the proper form of greeting in society; and (c) that the only legal marriages would be bicultural or biracial marriages! Wehrly et al. also emphasize the importance of bicultural or biracial marriages to the formation of a multicultural society. Changes in the legal system, demographic distribution, and population migration all favor the likelihood of increased multicultural and multiracial families in the future. The data supporting these trends are identified in detail by Wehrly et al.

According to Wehrly et al., we are living in a "transition period." By looking at the strengths and weaknesses of multiracial families we are looking at our own future, both locally and globally. The pretense that monocultural families are standard is less and less viable, as culturally defined special interest groups protect their identities more vigorously and as the need to pretend that "one size fits all" becomes less practical. The myths and stereotypes that attempted to impose monocultural perspectives on multiracial families are documented in detail by Wehrly et al. in the historical context where that imposition was demanded.

The current conditions and challenges demonstrate the up side of membership in a multiracial family, especially when we focus on the broad definition of culture, which includes the cultural categories of gay and lesbian populations (often not perceived as cultural groups). The practical emphasis of Wehrly et al.'s book comes through in examining specific issues within the multiracial family, including the perspectives of both adults and children. Eight popular theories of identity formation are applied to the multiracial family to identify patterns within the family that indicate positive growth and development.

The whole nature of family seems to be changing in both form and function with the increase of single-parent families, families that include unrelated persons, and homeless families, to name a few of the new forms that are increasing in number. The appropriate application of intervention and treatment competencies is addressed directly, as it must be adapted across the wide range of family alternatives. These competencies are applied to five case study examples, where theory is grounded in fact to help the reader see how these innovative ideas can be applied.

There are many positive features of Wehrly et al.'s book. The most important positive feature is the practicality of approaches that are presented so that when you, the reader, meet your client tomorrow morning, you will be better prepared to understand the multiracial context in which that client learned the assumptions that control his or her life. You will find a framework for understanding the family, which might otherwise be confusing. You will be more competent in helping clients manage the problems and opportunities facing them.

Paul Pedersen
University of Alabama at Birmingham

Acknowledgments

A host of people provided support and assistance in putting together this manuscript. First, we extend our gratitude to Paul Pedersen for suggesting that a proposal be submitted to the Multicultural Aspects of Counseling Series on the topic of counseling multiracial families. Our special appreciation goes to the Sage staff, particularly to Jim Nageotte, Kassie Gavrilis, Heidi Van Middlesworth, and Wendy Westgate. To Catherine Chilton, our copy editor, we extend our gratitude for her meticulous work. Collectively, this staff helped us to surmount the many barriers to completion of our book. Our special appreciation is extended to the numerous individuals from across the country who participated in our research interviews of multiracial individuals and couples. Several of their stories are included to help to make didactic content come alive.

Insightful suggestions for revision of early drafts of chapters of this book were offered by Paul Clark, Brian Wlazelek, Suzanne Nickeson, Sonia Assad, and Laurie Silverstein. Prepublication reviews by Paul Pedersen, Roger Herring, and Carolyn Tubbs gave valuable insight on ways to strengthen the book.

To these individuals we extend our sincere "thank you." Karen Hicks provided insurmountable assistance as we attempted to blend our voices into one, adding to the richness of this manuscript. To Susan Reffie, our clerical assistant, we extent our deepest gratitude and appreciation. Across over 800 miles she (amazingly) coordinated this project. Her understanding, patience, flexibility, and organizational and computer skills were astounding. To Melanie Rawlins, Chair of the Counselor Education and College Student Personnel Department at Western Illinois University, the senior author expresses special appreciation for providing graduate assistant support for locating relevant resource materials and conducting and transcribing taped interviews of multiracial individuals. Western Illinois University graduate assistants Joan Moore, Shannon Garrison, Janet McDaniel, and Amy Kreider participated in these endeavors.

The senior author also wishes to extend her special gratitude to her husband, Jim, for his half century of support to her as a nontraditional wife, mother, grandmother, career woman, and retiree.

Kelley Kenney would like to extend a thank you to her research colleague, Jo Cohen, for the tireless hours she put into their joint research venture on Black-White interracial marriage. Our work together offered a special contribution to the completion of this manuscript. To Connie Hwang, a thank you is expressed for her frequent delivery of interlibrary materials from Lehigh University. To her other colleagues at Kutztown University, Kelley would like to offer sincere appreciation for their support and encouragement through this process. To her husband, who also shared in the writing of this book, Kelley would like to express her genuine gratitude for his unending love, trust, and belief in her and in all that she does.

Mark Kenney would like to extend thanks to the Albright College Library staff, specifically Sandy Stump and Rose Mary Deegan, for their assistance in identifying relevant resources. He also extends his appreciation to Roger Herring and Cindy Yee for their response to his request for resource materials. To his wife, Kelley, he would like to express his deepest feelings of love and appreciation for all that she is and all that she means to him and their family.

Preface

Why This Book Was Written

Multiracial families (families in which at least one member of the family has a different racial heritage than the other member[s] of the family) comprise a rapidly growing part of the United States' population. There is still a dearth of counseling literature addressing this unique population.

Counseling Multiracial Families expands and updates the extant professional literature on counseling multiracial people and families. This book broadens the perspectives of helping service personnel on the historical background and the contemporary issues, needs, and strengths of the multiracial population. Culturally sensitive counseling interventions for work with multiracial individuals and families are presented.

Overview

Chapter 1 provides a historical overview of the concept of racial mixing in the United States. In so doing, the chapter provides an introduction to the multiracial population, along with definitions and demographic trends. Myths and stereotypes that have often been associated with this population are examined and discussed. Recommendations are made for the counseling profession in its work with this population.

Chapter 2 explores the lives of contemporary interracial couples, including gay and lesbian interracial couples. Issues and concerns that are salient to interracial couplings are discussed, with special emphasis on parenting and childrearing. Racial difference is considered for the possible significance it has on the dynamics of interracial relationships, and counseling implications are provided.

Chapter 3 discusses issues faced by multiracial individuals across the lifespan, reviews racial and ethnic reference group identity models for multiracial individuals, and translates biracial identity development theory into counseling practice with the children, adolescents, and adults in multiracial families.

Chapter 4 examines significant issues of other multiracial families. Included among these multiracial families are those that have become multiracial through foster home placement, cross-racial adoption from inside the United States, transracial adoption from foreign countries, and gay and lesbian multiracial partnering.

Chapter 5 examines current multicultural counseling competencies and discusses their relevance in working with the multiracial population. Approaches, interventions and strategies that may be effective with the multiracial population are presented.

Chapter 6 includes 5 case studies delineating application of content presented in the preceding chapters to work with an elementary-school-age biracial child, a transracially adopted college student, a multiracial adult, a multiracial couple, and a gay multiracial family.

1

Historical Overview

Multiracial Individuals, Interracial Couples, and Families

As this decade comes to a close and a new century begins, the counseling profession will need to be aware that there is an increasing number of individuals, couples, and families who are making different choices in regard to their racial identity, mate selection, and adoptive children. Individuals are deciding that they want to fully identify with all of their racial heritage. This idea was recently brought to the mainstream media's attention when sports figure Tiger Woods described himself as a "Cablinasian" to claim his Caucasian, Black, Indian and Asian ancestry (Eddings, 1997). With regard to couples, individuals in search of the ideal mate are now more willing to cross racial lines; once they have become a family, they are more willing to raise their children to accept all of their racial heritage. In addition, more individuals and couples are accepting the responsibility of raising children from racial backgrounds other than their own.

The counseling profession is just beginning to recognize the need to address the issues of persons who identify themselves as multiracial. Although the multicultural movement in counseling has expanded our understanding of monocultural and monoracial people, it has not, up to now, adequately addressed the unique needs and strengths of interracial couples and multiracial individuals and families (Wehrly, 1996). Previous research literature studying multiracial individuals, couples, and families is limited in the following ways: it looks at this population from the standpoint of deficits; it uses small sample sizes, clinical populations, and limited age groups; and it focuses on Black-White families and individuals (Root, 1997b; Thornton, 1996; Thornton & Wason, 1995). By focusing solely on the Black-White dynamic, this research concluded that all mixed heritage families and individuals were marginal because they were perceived to be doomed to a life of unresolvable conflict and identity confusion (Nakashima, 1992). Within the last decade, Asian Americans of mixed race have challenged this idea and have created their own theories and models of healthy multiracial identity development (Root, 1997b; Spickard, 1997). In recognition of these new voices and the complexity of this topic, this book broadens the scope of multiracialism by including multiracial people of various racial backgrounds, interracial couples, multiracial families of a variety of racial combinations and sexual orientations, and it examines the role of gender in relationships.

This chapter provides counselors with a larger context for understanding how the historical and sociopolitical environments throughout U.S. history have shaped our views of multiracial individuals, interracial couples, and multiracial families. It is the institutional racism of the past and the prejudicial attitudes of Whites of today that still deny the existence of a multiracial identity and discourage interracial marriage (Wehrly, 1996). In reaction to this oppression, some multiracial people have decided to identify monoracially, and some people of color have also voiced their opposition to interracial marriages within their community. But due to legal, social, and cultural events over the last 50 years, there has been an increase of interracial interactions in "schools, neighborhoods, places of entertainment, and work settings" (Wehrly, 1996, p. 4). With these increased interactions, the number of interracial marriages and domestic interracial birthrates of all groups has influenced the expansion of racial identity from the dichotomous "either/or" to a "both/and" view (Dalton, 1995). In addition, the most recent immigrants are bringing with them a different perspective on racial identity than most Americans. Because couples and individuals make up families, this chapter does not address the family as a separate topic. With regard to the uniqueness of adoptive and foster families, a more in-depth examination of these families is made in chapter 4.

Because of the importance and impact that race still has on our society, this book will use the terminology *interracial, multiracial,* and *transracial.* The term *interracial* is used to describe a relationship between two people from two or more socially designated racial groups (Root, 1996). The term *multiracial* is used to refer to an individual whose parents are of "two or more different socially designated racial heritages" (Root, 1996, p. xi). Biracial persons are included in this category. One type of multiracial family is defined as "two people of distinctly different racial heritages" and their offspring (Root, 1996, p. xi). An additional family type involves couples of same or different races who have transracially adopted. "Transracial indicates movement across racial boundaries and is sometimes synonymous with interracial and used in the context of adoption" (Root, 1996, p. xi). The term *family* is inclusive of all types of families, including single parents, two parents, heterosexual partners, homosexual partners, and grandparents raising children.

Finally, for historical purposes, there are two key terms to define: *antimiscegenation* and *hypodescendent*. "Antimiscegenation means against intermarriage or race-mixing"; "hypodescent refers to a social system that maintains the fiction of monoracial identification of individuals by assigning a racially mixed person to the racial group in their heritage that has the least social status" (Root, 1996, p. x).

The importance in understanding the complexity of this topic requires a further defining of important terms in this field of study. This involves providing demographics and reasons for the emerging importance of multiracialism, providing a historical overview of interracial marriage and multiracial identity, and discussing the myths and stereotypes about multiracial individuals and interracial couples.

The Mixing of the Races:
Present Time

The personal decisions of individuals, couples, and families to disregard societal norms about the meaning of race and racial identity has placed them in the middle of a public and volatile political issue. Individuals who want to claim their entire racial identity face the challenge of creating an identity that has never been supported by society and, therefore, have to defend their choice as healthy. Couples who make the decision to commit to an interracial relationship are still faced with potential societal or family opposition, even though there are no longer any legal prohibitions. All multiracial families are confronted by members of society, family members, and mental health professionals who have concerns about the likelihood of their children developing a healthy racial identity.

With these issues in mind, it is important for counselors to be aware of these disapproving opinions because the past professional literature only focused on the pathological aspects of multiracial individuals, couples, and families and did not address this population's experience with racial politics and racism (Root, 1997b). It is incumbent for all involved in the counseling process to understand how the larger society's views on race and race relations affect the private lives of these individuals, couples, and families. Furthermore, it is important for counselors to reflect upon their own values, beliefs, and views with regard to the individual's right to determine a multiracial identity, to the couple's right to love across perceived racial lines, and to the family's right to raise its children with a multiracial identity or to adopt transracially.

Definitions of Terms

Ethnicity, Culture, and Race

Defining the meanings of ethnicity, culture, and race will help to explain the use of the terms *interracial, multiracial,* and *transracial* in this book. This is an important consideration, as there is a lack of agreement on defining ethnicity, culture, and race in the field of psychology (Carter, 1995). Within the field, the debate ranges from believing that each term is distinctly different, to believing that each one is interrelated, to believing that one is more important than the others, to believing that race is meaningless.

Ethnicity refers to a certain group's characteristics with regard to food, work, relationships, celebrations, and rituals that separate them from the larger society (Cameron & Wycoff, 1998). Hays (1996a) notes that ethnic identity allows for a better understanding of an individual's unique heritage and value and is more informative than race. Therefore, some counseling professionals are currently using the term *multiethnic* in place of using any racial terminology (Herring, 1997). With this in mind, Hays (1996a) warns that counselors may need to further explore the distinction between cultural groups when there are broad ethnic categories such as Latino/Latina. Additionally, Robert T. Carter (1995) would counter that Americans interact and form relationships with each other based on their racial identities rather than their ethnic identities, because differences between people are seen more on a racial level than on an ethnic level.

Hays (1996a) defines culture as "all of the learned behaviors, beliefs, norms, and values that are held by a group of people and passed on from older members to newer members, at least in part to preserve the group"

(p. 333). This definition recognizes the existence of Muslim Americans who do not fit under any ethnic or racial category in the United States. Therefore, the term culture can be a more inclusive term, but if defined too broadly, it can allow individuals of the dominant culture to avoid the painful topic of oppression (Hays, 1996a; Locke, 1990). In using culture as the preeminent factor, Hays (1996a) proposed a "transcultural-specific" perspective that allows for the recognition of Muslim Americans but at the same time acknowledges the "power differentials" between the dominant group and minority groups.

In terms of race, there is general agreement among scholars that it does not have any biological significance describing personal characteristics but does have an important sociopolitical meaning in terms of group identity in our society (Hays, 1996a). Because of the historical practice in this country of using race to classify and to separate individuals by physical charac- teristics (i.e., skin color, hair texture, and features) and by assigning behav- ioral differences, race is still an important aspect of identity for many people (Carter, 1995). Historical legacy and the current sociopolitical meaning of race that multiracial persons experience has become part of the current racial political debate (Root, 1997b).

Although ethnicity and culture may be more informative and inclusive, the term race still holds significance in terms of creating the "marginalized" status of multiracial people in our society (Root, 1998). According to Root (1998), "race influences identity to some degree because physical appear- ance mediates acceptance and rejection of the individual by groups of his or her heritage and reflects a construction of reality that serves those who have desired resources and privileges" (p. 274). In addition, Carter (1995) contends that race and culture are interrelated despite being seen as two distinct entities.

Creation and Current Status
of Racial Categories

Although the first census count was taken in 1790, it was not until the 1870 census that the term *race* was first used to identify the categories of White, Colored, Chinese, and Indians ("The census snarl," 1997). During the late 19th and early 20th centuries, the United States government created a "mulatto" category and made efforts to count mulattoes separate from "pure Negroes" (Davis, 1991). This effort was abandoned in 1920, with Black referring to anyone with any Black ancestry (Davis, 1991). In 1960, the method of identifying one's racial category changed by having the head of the household decide the race of its members (Davis, 1991).

The next significant revision in racial categories occurred in 1977 with the issuance of Statistical Directive 15 by the Office of Management and Budget (Spencer, 1997). This directive designated four racial categories: "White, Black, Asian and Pacific Islander, and American Indian and Alaskan Native" (Spencer, 1997, p. 3). This change was requested by the government "to create a uniform standard of racial and ethnic classification in order to have 'compatible, nonduplicated, and exchangeable racial and ethnic data' among federal agencies" (Kalish, 1995, p. 2). One use of these data is "to monitor voting rights, and equal access for minorities in housing, education, and employment" (Eddings, 1997, p. 22). The data are also used "for tracking demographic shifts in the country, to address the requirements of civil rights laws, and to allocate government resources to meet the needs of the 'protected' minority groups that historically have been discriminated against" (Spencer, 1997, p. 3). In 1980, Hispanic was added as a category by the federal government "in order to identify and count all people of Spanish-speaking backgrounds with origins from the western hemisphere" (Galens, Sheets, & Young, 1995, p. 911).

In 1993, some Americans voiced their views that the 1980 racial categories needed to be changed for the 2000 census "to accurately reflect the diversity of the U.S. population" (Minghan, 1996, p. 144). Some changes presented to the government task force recommended the creation of separate categories for multiracial and monoracial people. In the case of monoracial groups, Hawaiians and Arab Americans felt that their category selection did not accurately describe their racial identity in regard to their relationship with the federal government (Spencer, 1997). The changes for monoracial groups for the 2000 census are that "Asians" will have a separate category from "Native Hawaiians or other Pacific Islanders," and the term "Latino" will appear with "Hispanic." For the multiracial groups, the change and compromise is that an individual may check as many racial categories as apply to him or her, but there will not be a separate multiracial category ("The census snarl," 1997).

Factors of Change That Increase the Interracial and Multiracial Population

According to Root (1997b), "the Civil Rights Movement, the repeal of antimiscegenation laws, integration of neighborhoods and a decrease in white opposition to interracial marriage constitute the climate in which multiracial people currently reach adulthood" (p. 32). Due to these events, and with an increase in interracial marriages, there has been a natural increase in the domestic multiracial birth rate. Another event has been the increase of immigrants with a different perspective on racial identity (Kalish, 1995). These two additional occurrences have contributed to the current blur in our society's view on the meaning of race (Kalish, 1995).

The most important event for interracial couples and multiracial individuals was the 1967 Supreme Court decision *Loving v. Virginia.* In June 1958, Mildred Jeters, an African American and Native American woman, and Richard Loving, a European American man, fell in love and were married in Washington, DC. Shortly after returning to their home in Caroline County, Virginia, they were arrested and convicted because their marriage was a violation of Virginia's antimiscegenation laws. A condition of the conviction was that they were forced to leave Caroline County and the state of Virginia, thus leaving family and friends behind. Their love for each other and desire to return to their home and family gave them the courage and determination to fight the conviction, taking their case all the way to the Supreme Court. On June 12th, 1967, the Supreme Court's decision banning antimiscegenation laws (which still existed in approximately 16 states) was handed down (Hollis, 1991). The court's decision stated that "the Virginia statutes violated both the Equal Protection and the 'due process clauses of the fourteenth amendment' " (Anderson, 1981, p. 79). The decision stated that under the equal protection clause, a state cannot discriminate against a group defined by race and that "under the Constitution, the freedom to marry, or not marry a person of another race, resides with the individual and cannot be infringed by the state" (Anderson, 1981, p. 80).

Interracial Marriages

Since the 1967 decision, the number of interracial marriages has increased from 150,000 in 1960 to more than one million in 1990 (Eddings, 1997). During this same time period, 74% of interracial marriages were between Whites and non-Blacks; only 24% were Black-White unions (Thornton & Wason, 1995). As indicated in Table 1.1, an increase in marriages between all groups continued in the 1990s, but there are two obvious statistical omissions from this table. The first is the lack of separate identification of marriages that occur between partners of Asian American, Native American, or Hawaiian/Pacific Islander but the other partner is not White, Black, or Hispanic; the second is the number of gay and lesbian interracial unions. Gay and lesbian couples are not counted by the U.S. Census Bureau because the bureau's definition of "unmarried couples" is described as "two unrelated adults of the opposite sex" (U.S. Bureau of the Census, 1998).

Table 1.1 Distribution of Married Couples of Same and Mixed Races and Origins, 1980 to 1997 (in thousands)

	1980	1990	1997
Non-Hispanic couples			
White-White	44,910	47,202	47,791
Black-Black	3,354	3,687	3,698
Black-White	167	211	311
White-other race	450	720	896
Black-other race	34	33	57
All other couples	799	1,401	1,912
Hispanic couples			
Hispanic-Hispanic	1,906	3,085	4,034
Hispanic-not Hispanic	891	1,193	1,662

SOURCE: U.S. Bureau of the Census (1998, pp. 20-509).

As demonstrated in Table 1.1, there were greater incidences of interracial marriages for all groups during the 1990s. In examining each racial group, it can be seen that Native Americans, Latinos, and Asian Americans are the most likely to intermarry; Blacks and Whites are least likely to intermarry (Grosz, 1997). The most common marriages occur between Whites and Asians; the least common combination is Black and Asian and "Other" (which includes Asian Indian, Native American, and Pacific Islander) (Grosz, 1997). According to Lind (1998), Native Americans have the highest rate of intermarriage. Because of the structure, rules, and policies in the United States military, which is more focused on equality and merit than is society outside the military, there is a greater occurrence of interracial marriages between most races than in the civilian population (Lind, 1998).

When considering gender, one finds that Latinas and Asian American and Native American women are more likely to be involved in interracial marriages, whereas Black and White men have a higher interracial marriage rate (Thornton & Wason, 1995). The highest rate of intermarriage occurs between White men and Asian women and the lowest rate is between White men and Black women (Grosz, 1997; Lind, 1998).

When examining geographic regions, one finds that the South and Midwest have the lowest percentages of interracial marriages; the Northeast and West have the highest rate (Grosz, 1997). Lind (1998) notes that "interracial marriages are more than twice as common in California (1 in 10 new couples)

Table 1.2 U.S. Interracial Births

	1978	*1992*
Black-White	21,400	55,900
Asian-White	21,013	42,033
Native American-White	12,860	21,819
Asian-Black	1,669	4,051
Native American-Black	557	1,454
Native American-Asian	379	789

SOURCE: Kalish (1995), p. 2.
NOTE: *Native American* includes American Indian, Eskimo, and Aleut.

as in the rest of the country (1 in 25 new couples)" (p. 38). There is a higher percentage of African American intermarriage in the West than in any other region (Tucker & Mitchell-Kernan, 1990). By looking at individual states who record these marriages, it can be seen that the states of Mississippi and West Virginia have the lowest rate of interracial marriages; Hawaii has the highest rate (Grosz, 1997).

An important and recent factor in the increase of interracial marriages is the gradual softening of opposition toward these marriages in the United States. A 1992 Gallop Poll found for the first time a slight majority of Americans who were opposed to antimiscegenation laws (Thornton & Wason, 1995). This change is reflected in a recent survey examining teenagers' attitudes toward interracial dating. In a comparison of a 1980 Gallup Poll and a 1997 Gallup Poll, more than double of teenagers of all races reported a willingness to date interracially (Peterson, 1997a). Although there were some stereotypical reasons for not dating interracially, the overall majority of respondents had a more open attitude toward such dating, except with Black-White unions, which are still viewed as the most difficult relationships (Peterson, 1997a).

Multiracial Individuals

With the increase in interracial marriages, there has also been an increase in racially mixed children. Beech (1996) stated that as of 1990 there were nearly 2 million children under 18 years old whom the census classified as "of a different race than one or both parents" (p. 56). According to Kalish (1995), "the National Center for Health Statistics shows that the interracial births more than doubled between 1978 and 1992, rising from about 63,700 to almost 133,200" (p. 1). These numbers could also be understated because the fathers' identities are not recorded for about 16% of U.S. births (Kalish, 1995). Lind (1998) noted that "millions of Hispanic mestizos and Black Americans who have European and Indian ancestors" are not included within this population (p. 38).

Table 1.2 shows the increase of interracial births between 1978 and 1992. As the table shows, there is an increase for all identified racial groups, and population projections do not indicate any slowing or reversal in this upward direction of growth (Root, 1997b). According to Thornton and Wason (1995), these children live primarily in California, Texas, New York, Illinois, Washington, and Hawaii and live mostly in Asian-White or Latino-White households.

Other increases in the multiracial population come from personal decisions of adults to redefine their private as well as public identities. This desire for change was publicly demonstrated in the census reports of the early 1990s. With the addition of the "other" category in 1990, multiracial people could exercise this choice for identity (Beech, 1996). According to the 1992 census, the "other" category grew more than any other category—by 45%, or 9.8 million people (Root, 1996).

Immigrants

Since the 1960s, the increase in the diversity and size of immigrant groups is due to changes in immigration laws that affect the number of interracial marriages and multiracial individuals. Snipp (1997) noted that the fastest growing segment of immigrant population in the 1960s and 1970s was from Mexico, Central and South America, and the Caribbean. The repeal of the anti-Asian legislation by the Immigration and Naturalization Act of 1965 leaves no doubt that it influenced the number of intermarriages during the early 1970s (Thornton, 1992).

Since 1980, there have been between 500,000 and 800,000 legal immigrants per year from Asia, Mexico, the Americas, and the Caribbean (Kalish, 1995). The fastest growing segment of the U.S. population in the 1980s was Asians (Snipp, 1997). Early Asian American immigrants were mainly Japanese, Chinese, and Filipino, but the most recent immigrants have been Korean, Vietnamese, Thai, Burmese, Laotian, Cambodian, Hmong, Asian Indian, and other Asians (Spickard, 1997). With the Amerasian Homecoming Act of 1987, many of the 40,000 to 50,000 Vietnamese Amerasians born to American military personnel were permitted to come to the United States (Root, 1998). As indicated in Table 1.3, the continued trend of immigration is from Asia, Mexico, the Americas, and the Caribbean.

Table 1.3   Immigrants, by Country of Birth: 1981 to 1996 (in thousands)

	1981 to 1990	*1991 to 1994*	*1996*
North America (total)	3,125.0	2,168.6	340.5
Mexico	1,653.3	1,397.9	163.6
Caribbean	892.7	441.8	116.8
Central America	458.7	226.7	44.3
Asia (total)	2,817.4	1,366.1	307.8
China	388.8	191.5	41.7
India	154.8	156.9	44.9
Philippines	495.3	241.6	55.9
Vietnam	401.4	234.0	42.1

SOURCE: U.S. Immigration and Naturalization Service data (U.S. Bureau of the Census, 1998).

As shown in Table 1.3, other people are migrating from countries where individuals may already consider themselves multiracial and have little understanding of the history of monoracial identity in this country. Between immigration and births, Latinos form nearly 10% of the United States population now and are predicted to become the largest minority by the year 2010 (Kalish, 1995). Furthermore, the Latino peoples may be of any race, and for them the "minority question" is less and less a "racial question" (Kalish, 1995). The difference in view with regard to race comes from the Latino experience of racial identity being more of a "social" category, as opposed to a legal concept that separates Whites from non-Whites in the United States (Rodriguez, Castro, Garcia, & Torres, 1991). Latinos see themselves as being similar in "essential nature," being varied in gradations and shades of color, and having more complex identity based upon "phenotype, social class, language, phenotypic variation within families, and neighborhood socialization" (Rodriguez et al., 1991, p. 33).

Some Asian immigrants have also brought a different perspective to this issue of racial identity. According to Root (1997b), "Filipinos have considered themselves as a mixed-race people" (p. 31). In addition, Vietnamese Amerasians have not found acceptance within their own community nor in White America because Asians are not always viewed as "real" Americans (Root, 1997b). Therefore, both the Latino and Amerasian immigrant populations have brought with them a similar view on the "fluidity" of identity as opposed to polarized monoracial identity created by the Black-White relational dynamic (Root, 1997b; Rodriguez et al., 1991).

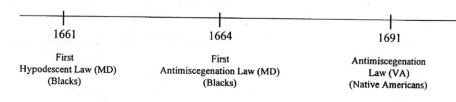

Figure 1.1. A Historical Overview Timeline: 1661 to 1819

The Mixing of Races:
A Historical Overview

A key reason for American society's difficulty with multiracialism is due to the historical relationship between Blacks and Whites. This relationship is based on the legal power and privilege of Whites over Blacks throughout a long portion of American history. With this understanding, the timeline is constructed on the basis of some of the important events that occurred between Whites and Blacks. It is not meant to be a definitive work regarding the experiences of all Americans. This section presents a historical account of the American people's support for the legal prohibition of interracial marriage by antimiscegenation laws, the denial of a multiracial identity due to the hypodescent statutes, and the passage of immigration laws to control the number of perceived "racially inferior" people coming to our shores. These three factors are explored in four time periods: 1660 to 1849, 1850 to 1919, 1920 to 1967, and 1968 to the present.

The first time period, 1660 to 1849, provides the backdrop for establishing antimiscegenation and hypodescent laws by early colonies and later by states with the two first groups identified as different by Whites: Blacks and Native Americans. From 1859 to 1919 and 1920 to 1967, there was a continuation of these groups' experiences with these laws. Furthermore, Asian Americans, Native Hawaiians and other Pacific Islanders, and Latinos had to deal not only with the antimiscegenation and hypodescent laws but with additional federal anti-immigration laws. Even though these later groups were discriminated against by the White legal system in a manner similar to Blacks, they each brought a different view about interracial relationships and racial identity and developed different relationships with Whites over time. The final time period, 1968 to the present, allows for a discussion of factors of change leading to the current status of interracial partners, multiracial individuals, and families.

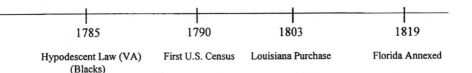

1785	1790	1803	1819
Hypodescent Law (VA) (Blacks)	First U.S. Census	Louisiana Purchase	Florida Annexed

1660 to 1849: Codification of Antimiscegenation and Identification

During this time period, the American economic and legal systems focused on how to maintain control over the two groups of people perceived to be most different from Whites: Blacks and Native Americans. There was a political need to create a myth of racial superiority and purity based on religious beliefs, and this was used to lay the foundation for the intolerance of interracial mixing and, eventually, for the legal prohibition of miscegenation within the English colonies (Frankenberg, 1995). The legal prohibition of interracial marriage and regulation of racial identity by colonial, state, and federal governments ensured the hierarchical structure of racial superiority by Whites as a means of maintaining their political and economic advantage over the African and Native American people (Frankenberg, 1995).

Antimiscegenation

In 1664, Maryland became the first colony to prohibit interracial marriages, specifically between "freeborn English women" and "Negro Slaves" (Pascoe, 1991). This is one example of the gender bias in antimiscegenation laws that focused more on preventing men of color from acquiring any access to the White society's power base, as opposed to preventing sexual relations between White men and women of other races (Pascoe, 1991). Pascoe makes this clear in her statement that interracial marriage "drew the strongest prohibitions and the most litigation, largely, I think, because marriage involved property obligations" (p. 7). Although Native Americans were included in the 1691 Virginia statute that forbade interracial marriage, Europeans did not discriminate against them by color as with the Africans but rather perceived them as different based on their cultural practices (Wilson, 1992).

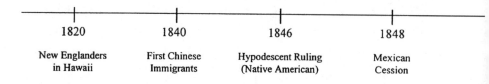

Figure 1.2. A Historical Overview Timeline: 1820 to 1882

Although these laws were enacted, marriages continued between Africans and Europeans, Native Americans and Africans, and Europeans and Native Americans—which meant that there already existed people of mixed race who were both free and slave (Nash, 1982; Williamson, 1980). In southern cities, there were marriages between indentured servants and enslaved Africans and between indentured servants and "free Africans" (Spickard, 1989). Up to and until the 1840s, there were some southern urban centers, such as Charleston, where marriages between mulattoes and White families took place (Davis, 1995).

In addition, the highest rate of intermixture of Native Americans, Blacks, and Whites involved the southeastern Indian groups known as the Five Civilized Tribes: Cherokee, Chickasaw, Choctaw, Creek, and Seminole (Wilson, 1992). These eastern tribes have descendents living today in the southeast and are identified as Indians: Jackson Whites, Brass Ankles, and Melungeons who were labeled as *triracial isolates* (Wilson, 1992). Although rare, there were even cases of marriages between European men and African women in New England during this time period (Spickard, 1989). One purpose of the antimiscegenation laws was to prohibit any union between people of different races and to prevent any further procreation of multiracial individuals (Fernandez, 1996).

Hypodescent

The regulation of racial identity largely came about with the increased need for Africans as slave labor; the White southern ruling class needed to codify behavior to maintain control over the larger African population (Spickard, 1989). The method used to identify distinction was skin color, and thus this was a factor used in determining the legal status of the individual as free or slave (Spickard, 1989). The first legal statute to determine racial identity as hypodescent was enacted in Maryland in 1661 (Frankenberg,

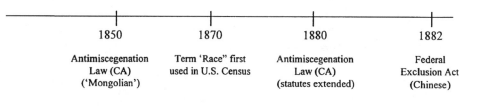

1850	1870	1880	1882
Antimiscegenation Law (CA) ('Mongolian')	Term 'Race" first used in U.S. Census	Antimiscegenation Law (CA) (statutes extended)	Federal Exclusion Act (Chinese)

1995). A second purpose in the creation of the "one drop rule" (hypodescent) was to determine one's racial identity to prevent unions between Black men and White women (Davis, 1995). Later, in post-Revolutionary times, "Virginia drew a genetic line by statute in 1785, defining a Negro as anyone with one-fourth or more African ancestry, a legal rule adopted generally in the upper South at the time" (Davis, 1995, p. 120). Thus, early on, the American legal system prevented "any notion of dual racial affiliations and formed a hierarchial system in which White is seen as superior and Black is seen as inferior" (Root, 1998, p. 265). This was reflected in the 1790 census, with the categories "Free White Males, Free White Females, Slaves, and other persons (including Free Blacks and Indians)" (Valentine, 1995, p. 47).

Native Americans were intermixing with each other before the arrival of the Europeans and Africans. The current research on "genetic markers" indicates a high degree of racial mixing among Native populations in North America, which was evident in pre-Columbian times (Jaimes, 1995). The identity concept of the one-drop rule or hypodescent is the antithesis of how American Indians or Native Americans determine their identity (Nash, 1982). It was not until the arrival of the Europeans that the concept of interracial mixing was used to "determine tribal membership or degrees of culture or acculturation" (Wilson, 1992). It was not until after the 1800s that Europeans viewed Indians as a darker race and labeled them as "red" (Wilson, 1992). Finally, in the mid-1800s, the American legal system decided in *United States v. Rogers* (1846) that for an individual to be identified as an Indian, he or she must show both cultural and biological links to a tribe (Wilson, 1992).

Immigration and Annexation

Between 1660 and 1849, immigration was still mainly a European experience, with the exception of African slaves. On the other hand, there were

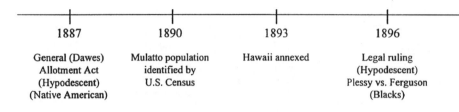

1887	1890	1893	1896
General (Dawes) Allotment Act (Hypodescent) (Native American)	Mulatto population identified by U.S. Census	Hawaii annexed	Legal ruling (Hypodescent) Plessy vs. Ferguson (Blacks)

Figure 1.3. A Historical Overview Timeline: 1887 to 1915

many land acquisitions due to American colonial expansionism. A significant act related to the issue of immigration was the ending of the legal slave trade in the United States in 1808 (Bailey, 1975). Another significant immigration event occurred in 1840 with the first wave of Chinese male laborers needed in California for mining and railway building.

With the land acquisition in the Louisiana Purchase of 1803, the United States absorbed a population of multiracial people referred to as Black Creoles, who "are mainly descendants of slaves or freed slaves and French colonists" (Levinson, 1994, p. 165). Although Black Creoles in New Orleans were forbidden to marry Blacks or Whites, some did anyway (Davis, 1995). With the annexation of Florida in 1819, the United States acquired a land inhabited by Spaniard, Native, free Black, and racially mixed populations (Bailey, 1975).

With American political and economic self-interest in continued westward expansion, New England missionaries arrived in Hawaii in 1820 and inter-racial marriages occurred between European or Chinese men and Hawaiian women (Spickard, 1989). The United States added 80,000 Mexican people of mixed heritage to the American culture with the annexation of Texas in 1845 and the territory gained from the Mexican cession of 1848 (Galens et al., 1995).

1850 to 1919: Solidification of Legal Standards and Monoracial Identity

During this time, and in some regions, White America became more vigilant in prohibiting new immigrants and conquered peoples from marry-ing interracially, as well as in clearly defining who was not White. According to Pascoe (1991), "Although most northern states repealed their prohibitions after the Civil War, in the South and the West, laws against miscegenation

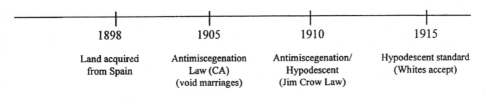

1898	1905	1910	1915
Land acquired from Spain	Antimiscegenation Law (CA) (void marriages)	Antimiscegenation/ Hypodescent (Jim Crow Law)	Hypodescent standard (Whites accept)

remained in force through much of the twentieth century" (p. 6). The focus and the philosophies of state legislatures during this time period were to eliminate any potential existence and recognition of multiracial people. This was done by identifying and adding non-White people to existing anti-miscegenation laws and by making it virtually impossible for anyone with any non-White ancestry ever to be considered White. These legislative actions supported Whites' continued desire to exclude non-Whites from accessing any economic or political power within their region (Frankenberg, 1995). In addition, by looking at racial identity as "pure" or "impure" and eliminating any "hybridity" option, Whites could continue to determine who could have access to power both economically and politically in the entire country (Nakashima, 1992).

Antimiscegenation

With the presence of Native Americans and the increase of Mexicans and Asians in the West, antimiscegenation laws that included these groups were passed in California and other western states in the 1850s (Frankenberg, 1995). Besides the traditional Black-White prohibition, groups were added in this order: Native Americans, Chinese, Japanese, and then the term "Mongolian" was created to cover both Chinese and Japanese people (Pascoe, 1991).

These California statutes were extended in the 1880s and "prohibited the issuance of a license authorizing the marriages of a white person with a Negro, Mulatto or Mongolian" (Frankenberg, 1995). Toward the end of 19th century, western states added other groups to their antimiscegenation laws as they became a threat to the status quo of White society: Filipinos, Hawaiians, and Hindus (Pascoe, 1991). In addition, Pascoe found that anti-miscegenation laws were applied most stringently to groups of Chinese,

Japanese, and Filipinos because it was thought that these men of color were most likely to marry White women. The law was applied least stringently to Native American women and Latinas because it was thought that they were most likely to marry White men (Pascoe, 1991). For example, due to the land-owning privilege of Mexican women, it became socially acceptable for White males to marry these women (Allman, 1996). While all these other groups were being prevented from marrying Whites, Native Americans continued to grow as a multiracial population, as reflected in the 1910 census, which "enumerated 40 percent" of the population as of mixed race (Snipp, 1997).

During the Reconstruction Era and into the early 20th century, there was a decrease of Black-White sexual contact in the South due to the heightened animosity caused by the Civil War. During this time, marriages between African Americans and European Americans were infrequent and were mainly in the northern and western regions (Spickard, 1989).

Hypodescent

Between 1850 and 1910, the Census Bureau made changes in categories nearly every decade to try to identify new non-White immigrants. From 1870 to 1890, the Census Bureau attempted to identify and count the mulatto or "Black/White" population separately from Blacks. This was in direct contradiction to what was happening in southern, western, and federal legislatures, which were passing laws that made it more difficult for a person to be identified as "White."

Southern legislatures began to write stronger antimiscegenation laws, forbidding marriages between Whites and anyone of Black ancestry to prevent any increase in the multiracial population. In addition, Davis (1995) found that southern states began to write limiting legal definitions of Black persons who were of one fourth, one eighth, or another fraction of Black ancestry. Based on White southern rejection of some intermediate status, mulattoes began to identify with the African population as opposed to the "almost White" group (Davis, 1995).

On the federal level, the 1896 Supreme Court decision of *Plessy v. Ferguson* served to legitimize the Jim Crow laws of the South that advocated "separate but equal." According to Davis (1995), "The Supreme Court briefly took judicial notice of the definition of a 'Negro' as a person with any known black ancestry" (p. 122). In addition, Davis stated that "Plessy v. Ferguson shows how the one-drop rule was used to strengthen white domination of blacks" (p. 122).

By 1910, in the South, Jim Crow laws clearly defined who was a Negro by the one-drop rule and strengthened the antimiscegenation laws. Jim Crow laws were a codified means to remove all citizenship rights that African Americans gained in the Reconstruction period. According to Davis (1995), "by 1915, the one-drop rule had become universally backed by Whites in the South and the North" (p. 122).

As noted in the mulatto experience in the South, the state of California tried to make the Chinese problem disappear (Frankenberg, 1995). In 1905, the California law was strengthened to declare existing interracial marriages void (Frankenberg, 1995). In 1906, laws were enacted dealing with immigration controls and antimiscegenation with regard to Japanese laborers (Frankenberg, 1995). According to Frankenberg, these laws were enacted to prevent "mongrelization as the dreaded outcome of interracial sexuality and procreation" (p. 73).

The General (Dawes) Allotment Act of 1887 "mandated the requirement that all eligible Indian individuals for allotments must be at least one half or more Indian blood" (Jaimes, 1995, p. 136). This "blood quantum" method of identification is in direct contrast to some Native American tribes' system of identifying members (Jaimes, 1995). This act also had a gender aspect because White males could acquire their Native American wife's land and have it taken from her tribal parcel (Jaimes, 1995). As with the situation with Mexican women, this is further evidence of the use of White male privilege to manipulate the system to their advantage and prevent others from accessing power.

Immigration and Annexation

In terms of immigration laws, the 1882 Federal Exclusion Act prevented any further immigration of Chinese laborers, and the 1884 act extended this to exclude the wives of Chinese male immigrants (Frankenberg, 1995). In 1913, California passed the Alien Land Laws as a means of preventing Chinese and Japanese people from owning land and thus forcing some of them to return to their homelands (Spickard, 1989).

In 1893, the United States annexed Hawaii with its populations of Native Hawaiians, Chinese, Japanese, Filipinos, and multiracial people. In 1898, the United States acquired the following lands: Guam, Puerto Rico, the Philippines, and Cuba. Puerto Ricans were granted United States citizenship in 1917. This is significant because Puerto Ricans have a more complex understanding of racial difference based upon phenotype, not the simple American hypodescent system of being one race or the other (Falcon, 1995).

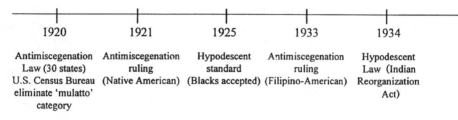

Figure 1.4. A Historical Overview Timeline: 1920 to 1948

1920 to 1967: Time of Invisibility and Quiet Change

During this time period, both the state and federal governments began to write stricter, well-defined antimiscegenation and hypodescent laws. At the same time, Americans began to adopt the concept of a monoracial identity, and the rate of interracial marriage decreased. The White legal system had achieved its goal of constructing the concept of "racial purity" and, therefore, clearly distinguished the "superior" from the "inferior." An outcome of this situation was the beginning of unification and pride of identity for people of color. This created a time of invisibility for people of multiracial identity because their only choice was to identify with the population of color.

During this same time period, there were four significant events that laid the foundation for change. First, in 1948, the California Supreme Court ruled that a state's antimiscegenation law was unconstitutional (Frankenberg, 1995). Secondly, the 1954 Supreme Court decision of *Brown v. the Board of Education* began the process of removing the legal barriers of racial separation in education and setting the stage for integration in the larger society (Spickard, 1989). Thirdly, in 1958, Mildred Jeter and Richard Loving were married and then arrested in Caroline County, Virginia, for violating that state's antimiscegenation law. Finally, in 1959, Hawaii, with its large interracial and multiracial population, was granted statehood but still had to accept the U.S. Census Bureau's system of monoracial classification (Davis, 1995).

Antimiscegenation

By 1920, 30 of the 48 states had antimiscegenation laws, which were enforced until after World War II (Spickard, 1989). Usually, these laws declared Black-White marriages criminal, null, and void. Parties were fined up to $1,000 and sentenced to prison for 10 years or more (Spickard, 1989). Incidently, during this period of time, interracial marriages between Blacks

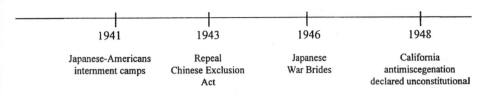

1941	1943	1946	1948
Japanese-Americans internment camps	Repeal Chinese Exclusion Act	Japanese War Brides	California antimiscegenation declared unconstitutional

and Whites increased from 1% to slightly over 1% (Spickard, 1989). And, although the African American community did not look favorably on these relationships, it did show a certain degree of tolerance by allowing these couples to live on the fringes of African American communities (Spickard, 1989).

In addition, western courts were deciding that long-term interracial marriages were invalid, as in the 1921 Oregon case of *In re Paquet's Estate*. The Native American wife lost her husband's estate to her brother-in-law because of the broad language of the miscegenation law prohibiting marriage between "any white person and any Negro, Chinese or any person having one fourth or more negro, Chinese, or Kanaka blood, or any person having more than one half Indian blood" (Pascoe, 1991, p. 7). Although she claimed that she had the same rights as Whites, the Oregon Supreme court decided that "the statute did not discriminate against Native Americans because . . . 'it applies alike to all persons, either white, negroes, Chinese, Kanakas or Indians' " (Pascoe, 1991, p. 8).

Upon the examination of the Los Angeles county marriage records from 1924 to 1933, it was found that the Japanese had the lowest rate of intermarriage, and the following groups had outmarried at a higher rate: African Americans, Chinese, Native Americans, and Filipinos (Spickard, 1989). In 1933, a California judge decided that a Filipino man could marry a White woman because he did not fit the description of a "Mongolian" but rather "Malays" (Pascoe, 1991). The California legislature responded by adding "Malays" to their antimiscegenation law (Pascoe, 1991).

In Hawaii, the rate of interracial marriage between mainland male servicemen and island women was on the rise until 1945 (Spickard, 1989). At the same time in California, the Japanese-American internment camps led to a deep reduction of interracial marriage involving Japanese Americans that lasted well into the 1950s (Spickard, 1989). An exception to this situation

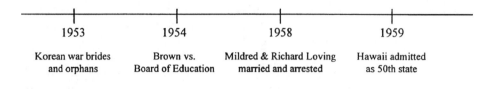

Figure 1.5. A Historical Overview Timeline: 1952 to 1967

was the increase of Japanese brought home by the American troops, as well as Korean war brides as a result of the Korean conflict in the early 1950s. Ironically, "prior to 1960, most Asian-Americans were opposed to intermarriage and mixed children" (Spickard, 1997, p. 45).

Hypodescent

In terms of racial identity, this time period continued to solidify the either/or concept of identity that was evident in the way social norms and legal definitions became very similar. Although it became very clear who was Black and who was White, other multiracial people of color were having a very different experience.

A critical government action in 1920 was the elimination of the mulatto category by the U.S. Census Bureau. The U.S. Census Bureau discontinued the practice of identifying people as mixed race because the person's race was determined on the external appearance of the individual by each census taker (Williamson, 1980). The problem with this method of "eyeballing" was that the U.S. Census Bureau did not have a mutually agreed-on standard by which to classify an individual as mulatto (Williamson, 1980). Therefore, the U.S. Census Bureau required each individual to be identified as a member of a single race, with no provision for mixed-race ancestries (Davis, 1995). Consequently, in the 1920s, internal miscegenation began between mulattoes and Blacks, resulting in everyone identifying themselves as Black despite their interracial past (Williamson, 1980). "By 1925, the American Black community, including most mulattoes, firmly supported the one-drop rule" (Davis, 1995, p. 123).

The legal conflicts with the identity of Native Americans and Asian Americans and their social acceptance by others was not as settled as in the Black community. In the case of Native Americans, Congress mandated

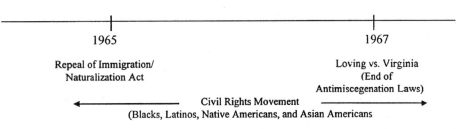

1965

Repeal of Immigration/
Naturalization Act

1967

Loving vs. Virginia
(End of
Antimiscegenation Laws)

Civil Rights Movement

(Blacks, Latinos, Native Americans, and Asian Americans

"civil rights codes" in the Protection of Indians and Conservation of Resources Act constitutions of 1934 (Jaimes, 1995). This act changed the more
traditional matrilineal descendence within nations to the patrilineal descendence model of Whites (Jaimes, 1995). This resulted in the males of a tribe
having the power to decide who is a member of their nation as opposed to
tracing relationships through the mother's ancestry (Jaimes, 1995). The
Protection of Indians Act, like the Dawes Act, was another example of abuse
of federal power to determine the identity of native peoples instead of
allowing each nation to make that decision (Jaimes, 1995). Although the
Native American population is more likely to accept their multiracial population, the federal government was more interested in denying multiracial
Indians' existence, to reduce the Native Americans' political and economic
power (Snipp, 1997).

In the case of multiracial Asian Americans, experiences varied from being
totally ignored to being forcibly rejected. Both the White and Asian communities determine the individual's racial identity and acceptance, as opposed
to the individual determining his or her own identity and being able to expect
acceptance in whichever community he or she chooses (Spickard, 1997). In
the 1930s, Chinese Hawaiians were the largest group of Amerasians, but they
were more accepted in the Hawaiian community than in the Chinese community (Spickard, 1997). During this same period, Japanese Americans did
not accept most multiracial people in their community (Spickard, 1997).
Whites also opposed interracial marriages with Asians, but because Amerasians were such a small segment of society, Whites "could ignore such
individuals and let them slide by on the margins of white society" (Spickard,
1997, p. 46). As Spickard points out, "The common thread is that nearly all
mixed racial people of Asian descent prior to the 1960s had to make their
way outside of Asian American communities, for Asian communities would
not have them" (p. 49).

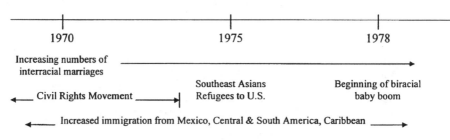

Figure 1.6. A Historical Overview Timeline: 1970 to 1989

Immigration

During this time of difficulty for interracial couples and multiracial people, events occurred in immigration that would foreshadow the beginnings
of change for the second half of the 20th century. The first event was the
repeal of the Chinese American Exclusion Act in 1943. Besides the influx of
Japanese war brides and Korean war brides, there were also Korean orphans
of mixed heritage and Filipino wives and children of American fathers
returning to the United States (Root, 1998). This is the start of the 50-year
presence of the American military in the Pacific Rim that would result in an
increase in relationships between Asian women and (primarily) male American soldiers (Root, 1998).

1968 to the Present: Time for Self-Determination

The Lovings' decision to challenge the antimiscegenation laws of Virginia
was motivated by their personal desire to return to their birthplace and
families. The Civil Rights Movements, the Women's Movement, and the Gay
Rights Movement share a personal component in wanting to challenge the
law, but they also possess a larger political agenda: to create legislative law
to secure their members' rights in this society. This section will discuss how
these movements shaped the contemporary multiracial movement. Political
motivation is the key difference between how the antimiscegenation laws
ended and how some people who want a separate multiracial identity sought
to change Americans' views on racial identity.

Antimiscegenation

There was a gradual increase in interracial marriages and an acceptance
of their existence during this time period. As expressed by Spickard (1997),

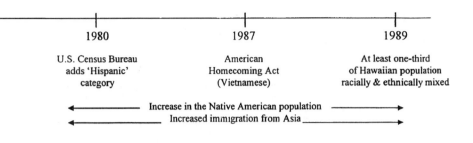

"by the 1970s, the numbers of Chinese and Japanese who married outside their respective groups and then had children was so large that Asian American communities were forced to begin to come to terms and accept the existence of mixed people" (p. 49). During this same period, according to Snipp (1997), the "American Indian rate of intermarriage has increased due to urbanization and to erosion of ethnic boundaries" (p. 677). Even with the recent relational tensions between Blacks and Whites, the number of Black-White marriages increased from 51,000 in 1960 to 311,000 in 1997 (Lind, 1998). In addition, the current rate of intermarriage among ethnic groups in Hawaii is still a significant portion of total marriages (Davis, 1995). Therefore, Hawaii could be the best alternative model with regard to how the mainland United States could become more accepting of this growing phenomenon.

There is currently a compelling need to study couples in which neither partner is White. Wilson (1992) states that "there are many instances of Filipino-Native American as well as other Asian-American-Native American interracial couples and multiracial offspring in California, but no scholarly or popular notice" (p. 122). This is another example of an underlying racism in the study of interracial marriage by primarily focusing on White-color relationships and not on color-color relationships (Wilson, 1992). The lack of study on the latter topic is another example of a serious omission in "an important social and cultural phenomenon in American history" (Wilson, 1992, p. 110).

Hypodescent

The various people's movements of the 1960s and 1970s (e.g., Black Power, Chicano, Asian American, and Native American) empowered individuals to determine their own cultural meaning and self-definition. The experience of multiracial people in each of these movements varied from

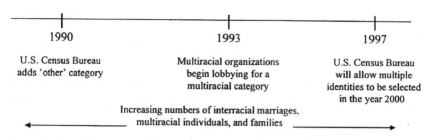

Figure 1.7. A Historical Overview Timeline: 1990 to 1997

group to group, and therefore the acceptance of multiracial identity varied from group to group.

The Black Power or "Soul" movement of the 1960s again united monoracially to fight for the rights of Blacks even though there was an acknowledgment of their multiracial identity history (Williamson, 1980). In the Chicano Movement, the monoracial-multiracial identity issue was not an issue because the majority of the participants were of mixed-race heritage (Galens et al., 1995). This was a similar theme within the Native American movement, as identity was based more on participation and kinship than on biological determination (Snipp, 1997).

Based on the historical experience of the African American community with hypodescent statutes, some Blacks are not in complete agreement with this concept of a multiracial identity or category (Spencer, 1997). After the Native American community, the Black community has the next highest percentage of people with a multiracial heritage. Therefore, a multiracial category could seriously undermine Black racial identity and break up Black solidarity (Spencer, 1997). Spencer (1997) also acknowledges that a more open acceptance of interracial relationships and multiracial individuals of African heritage might actually strengthen the Black community by preventing mixed-race people from supporting a separate multiracial category.

Since 1960, there has been a phenomenal growth in the Native American population (Snipp, 1997). Persons with any Native American ancestry are choosing to identify themselves as Native Americans instead of disappearing altogether into White society (Snipp, 1997). Even individuals of minimal Native American ancestry and high acculturation have a desire to have some connection with their Native American identity. There are Native American people who advocate self-identification along with involvement in the Native American community and with acceptance of a bicultural identity (Wilson, 1992). The federal government is still trying to control Native American identity, as evidenced by the *Indian Arts & Crafts Act of 1990,* which continues the practice of preventing Native Americans from determining their own identity criteria (Jaimes, 1995).

Multiracial Asian Americans had a different experience with the Asian American movement. "Those involved in the Asian American movement of the 60s and 70s seldom had a place for people of multiple ancestry or their distinctive issues" (Spickard, 1997, p. 49). According to Spickard, this has led multiracial Asian Americans to believe that to "embrace both (or all) parts of one's identity is a healthier situation than to cling to one and pretend that the other does not exist and to adopt what Amy Iwasaki Mass calls 'situational ethnicity' " (p. 51). "Situational ethnicity" is a more fluid way of being because identity depends on one's feelings in relationship to the people around the individual at that particular moment: Whites, Blacks, Latinos, or Asians (Spickard, 1997, p. 50).

In the 1980 census, two thirds of the people of Hawaii designated "other" as their racial identity (Davis, 1995). By 1989, racially and ethnically mixed people were the largest segment of the Hawaiian population—at least one third (Davis, 1995). Racially mixed people in Hawaii, rather than being assigned membership in any parent group, are perceived and respected as persons with roots in two or more ancestral groups (Davis, 1995). The implicit rule has been that mixed-race persons are to be accepted as such and treated as equals by all racial and ethnic groups (Davis, 1995). According to Haunani Kay Trask, "We (the Native Hawaiians) are the only populations that are defined racially on the Islands. . . . We traditionally determined our membership by genealogy that is connected with the land and which is different than race" (Jaimes, 1995, p. 141).

In response to these changing views on racial identity, there have been political, academic, and support organizations throughout the United States to provide information, to conduct research, and to promote a view of multiracial people that is an alternative to the stereotypical pathologized view of a multiracial person as one who does not fit into the mutually exclusive racial categories (Thornton & Wason, 1995). Two national multiracial organizations, the Association of MultiEthnic Americans and Project RACE (Reclassify All Children Equally), were active in lobbying the government to add a multiracial category to the 2000 census (Fernandez, 1996; Graham, 1996). Still others formed organizations like the Amerasian League in West Los Angeles to provide a place for the study of multiraciality (Spickard, 1997). Others have formed regional support groups to allow families and individuals to gather for social purposes and to provide informational newsletters on multiracial matters and concerns.

Myths and Stereotypes Regarding Interracial Couples and Mulitiracial Individuals

Myths and stereotypes were developed by the early Europeans and later by White Americans as a means to socially prevent interracial marriages and to stigmatize their offspring. The former is still evident in the socialized messages that we receive about the perceived "superiority" and "inferiority" of an individual based upon skin color. The latter factor surfaces in the current-day question asked of interracial couples: "What about the children?" (Root, 1998).

Interracial Couples

According to Frankenberg (1995), there is still substantial opposition to interracial marriage, but there are some "modern" reasons based on the "assumptions of total difference between members of different racial groups" (p. 77). Frankenberg (1995) identifies seven elements in the current discourse against interracial relationships:

> racialized stereotyping of masculinity, racialized stereotyping of femininity, the transgression of fixed racial or cultural boundaries, the inherently doomed "mixed" race child, the "fixed" meaning of race, the "absoluteness" of culture, and the hierarchical thinking in regard to the nature of race and culture. (p. 77)

Psychological Stereotypes

Spickard (1989) reports that myths have been used to explain interracial marriages. The underlying themes of these myths suggest pathological thinking or abnormal behavior on the part of one or both of the partners. A major conclusion drawn about these couples is that their relationships are based solely on unhealthy motives. Themes that have emerged suggest that people who marry interracially are motivated by racial self-hatred, a desire for the exotic, rebellion toward family, or a desire to show liberal views of race relations (Spickard, 1989). Research with these conclusions has been criticized for being of questionable scientific validity.

Besides these myths, the "Exchange Theory" (Levinson, 1995) has been proposed. The basic concept is that "people of color who marry Whites are trying to 'raise' themselves economically, socially, and racially; intermarriage and multiracial people represent the loss or the 'dilution' of distinct ethnic and racial groups; and mixed-race people and their families have dubious political and social loyalties" (Nakashima, 1992, p. 165).

Sexual Stereotypes

Also, the issues of race and gender intersect when it comes to stereotyping the behavior of women and men of color. In terms of sexual behavior, both women and men of color are described as "excessive, animalistic, or exotic in contrast to the ostensibly restrained or 'civilized' sexuality of White women and men" (Frankenberg, 1995, p. 75). According to Spickard (1989), Whites view Black women "as unnaturally passionate, attractive, easily exploitable sex objects and possessing exceptional sexual capabilities and enthusiasm" (p. 238). In sharp contrast, Black men are viewed as "exceptionally virile, promiscuous, dangerous, less than human, violent and rapacious" (Spickard, 1989, p. 238). In contrast, Asians are assigned a less threatening image by White Americans. For example, according to Frankenberg (1995), Asian men are "less sexually threatening and more acceptable than African American men" (p. 76). Asian women, particularly during the Second World War, were seen as "exotic, erotic creatures able to please men in special ways" (Spickard, 1989, p. 40).

Multiracial Individuals

According to Cynthia Nakashima (1992), there are two factors used to describe multiracial people negatively: biological and sociocultural reasoning. Biological reasoning has to do with the perception that it is "unnatural to mix the races" and "that intermarriage 'lowers' the biological superiority of the White race" (Nakashima, 1992, p. 165). The sociocultural reasoning has to do with the multiracial person's experience as "socially/culturally marginal" (Nakashima, 1992). Again, the historical events and political meanings of race have affected the psychological issue of multiracial identity.

Psychological Stereotypes

The purpose behind creating the myths about multiracial people on a biological basis was to:

keep the dominant "White race" pure, separate, and superior, and in power by
both discouraging White people from marrying and/or having children with
people of color and by making sure that all of these people could not claim
any privilege from their European ancestry. (Nakashima, 1992, p. 165)

Nakashima (1992) further stated that:

They were also (and, to some extent, still are) characterized as depressive,
moody, discontented, irrational, impulsive, fickle, criminal, chronically confused, emotionally unstable, constantly nervous, and ruled by their passions—
all because of an internal disharmony between the genetically determined
characters of their parent races. (p. 167)

This biological disharmony was then tied to the sociocultural myth
making. The key myth is that the "multiracial person was doomed to a life
of conflicting cultures and unfulfilled desires to be one or the other"
(Nakashima, 1992, p. 165). The inability to resolve this conflict and non-
acceptance from either racial group would result in the person being "marginalized and an outcast" (Nakashima, 1992, p. 171). As with the case of
interracial couples, Root (1998) noted that these pathologies were based on
research that was of questionable quality and validity.

Sexual Stereotypes

All multiracial people have been stereotypically identified as "sexually
immoral and out of control" (Nakashima, 1992, p. 168). Because multiracial
people are the offspring of an "immoral" union, they are expected to be
immoral as well as psychologically or socially abnormal (Nakashima, 1992).
Gender also plays a role: "multiracial women are particularly vulnerable to
internalizing the oppressive expectations of the exotic woman because of
society's socialization to the importance of physical appearance, mixed
messages of women's sexuality, and the oppressive beliefs about multiracial
women's sexuality" (Root, 1998, p. 282). The sexuality myths are also
related to the physical attractiveness stereotype of multiracial people
(Nakashima, 1992). Over time, it has been noted that "The idea that multiracial people are beautiful and handsome is one of the most persistent and
commonly accepted stereotypes both historically and contemporarily"
(Nakashima, 1992, p. 169).

Summary

This chapter provided an overview of the multiracial experience in the United States. The reason that a multiracial identity has not existed in this country was the creation of a hierarchical relationship between Whites and Blacks through antimiscegenation laws and hypodescent statutes. Although these laws no longer exist, they still shaped our current social construct of racial identity. Counselors need to realize that Native Americans, Asian Americans, Latinos, and Hawaiians have had a very different view on the construct of racial identity. Some domestic multiracial groups, specifically multiracial Asian Americans, have developed their own healthy models of identity, but Native Americans, Latinos, and Hawaiians have never really accepted the American concept of racial identity. In addition, now that individuals will be able to select more than one racial category in the 2000 census, the whole concept of hypodescent has been changed forever.

With the projected increase of domestic multiracial births and of immigrants with a different perspective on racial identity, there is going to be continued growth in a population that will not accept the current method of racial identification. In addition, the continued opportunities of interactions between people of various racial backgrounds will be likely to influence the continued growth of interracial unions. Besides the expansion of the meanings of *interracial, multiracial,* and *transracial* beyond the Black-White dynamic, there is a need to be more inclusive of gays and lesbians when discussing couples and families. Counselors will need to assess their own views on this population as well as be able to assess its the needs, strengths, and diversity. Multiracialists will most likely attempt to lobby for a multiracial category for the 2010 census, so this topic will remain a relevant issue in our society. Therefore, it is paramount for counseling professionals to increase their knowledge and broaden their understanding of interracial couples, multiracial individuals, and their families.

2

Interracial Marriage

Current Conditions and Challenges

This chapter is an exploration of the lives of contemporary interracial married couples based on recent literature on interracial marriage. Results of recent research on the topic, including a study conducted by Kelley Kenney and Jo Cohen that began in 1992, are provided. Because of the limited amount of professional literature available on the various combinations of interracial marriages that exist in the United States, a portion of the information presented in this chapter is based on anecdotal discussions with various interracial couples who expressed a willingness to share their experiences. In addition, Kelley Kenney shares her own experiences as a partner in an interracial marriage (all uses of "I" in this chapter refer to Kelley Kenney).

Special emphasis is placed on issues of parenting and child rearing specifically related to positive self-concept and identity development. Salient social and cultural issues associated with the child rearing of multiracial children is also explored. Attention is also given to interracial gay and lesbian couples, particularly in light of the number of these couples that currently exist and who live in exclusive, monogamous, and even married partnerships.

Finally, a discussion of the significance and insignificance of racial differences for interracial couples is explored. A tenet that I am currently developing on racial and cultural empathy is introduced, and implications for counseling interracial couples are presented.

The Lives of Contemporary Interracial Married Couples

Despite the decrease of legal barriers to interracial marriage that occurred as the result of the 1967 *Loving v. Virginia* Supreme Court decision, marriage across racial lines continues to be a lifestyle that is subject to considerable mixed reaction. Couples involved in interracial relationships in general are faced with questions, stares, discrimination, inappropriate comments, and often rejection (Nash, 1997). Much of the scrutiny of these relationships seems to be related to theories discussed in Chapter 1. These theories are representative of the myths and stereotypes that have long been associated with these unions and that cut across all racial lines.

Lack of acceptance on the part of persons from both races is still a prevalent issue for many interracial couples (Kayleng, 1998; Paset & Taylor, 1991; Simpson & Yinger, 1985), as are strong sentiments against racial mixing (Davidson, 1992). Prejudicial attitudes, discrimination, and rejection can be a source of difficulty for some couples, particularly as they attempt to deal with typical relational concerns that face even same-race couples, such as finances (Solsberry, 1994). A variety of behaviors, ranging from overt acts of violence to more covert expressions of discouragement (Root, 1994), emanate from this lack of acceptance. The degree of difficulty experienced by an interracial couple varies based on the couple's socioeconomic level, educational background, and the community in which they live (Solsberry, 1994).

In interracial relationships involving White women, the level of difficulty may also vary based on the racial background of the male (Frankenberg, 1995). For example, Asian males have been mentioned as being less sexually threatening in our society. Hence, a relationship between an Asian male and White female is likely to provoke less resentment. In fact, it is suggested that Latinos and Asian men are more acceptable than Black men as partners for White women. Further, Yasinski (1998) discusses the extent to which negative attitudes of the White community are reminiscent of racial purity concerns; also, some persons of color believe that intermarriage is inconsistent with the development of a sense of community. Azoulay (1997) indicates that one of the primary reactions to individuals who marry out of the community in both the Jewish and the Black communities is a charge of disloyalty. This charge can be attributed to an interest in holding on to a sense of group solidarity, an attitude resulting from the history of racism and oppression experienced by both of these groups.

Most of the research literature on couples in interracial marriages deals with marriages in which one partner is of African American background and the other is of European American background. Although this coupling represents the smallest proportion of interracial married couples in the United States, it is by far the most controversial and therefore subject to the most negative and racist attitudes (Brown, 1987; Johnson, 1991; Robinson & Howard-Hamilton, 1994). Isolation and alienation from family, friends, and neighbors have been reported as some of the stressors felt by couples in Black-White marriages (Hedgeman, 1987). Unions between Black males and White females, in particular, continue to meet with intense hostility (Frankenberg, 1995).

The experiences of these couples can result in feelings of social, emotional, psychological, or even physical vulnerability (Brown, 1987), but for many couples, the relationship serves as an interpersonal growth opportunity the partners might never have experienced otherwise (Solsberry, 1994). In examining issues related to making a commitment to marry interracially, Kenney and Cohen (1998) found that for many of the 80 Black-White couples in their sample, the establishment of a strong sense of individual personal security and security as a couple made them feel more bonded and willing and able to face challenges. The establishment of positive self-esteem, both individually and as a couple, serves as a way of countering feelings of vulnerability. Nash (1997) further emphasizes the significance of positive self-esteem in discussing issues of coping in interracial dating relationships. Healthy levels of self-esteem and self-confidence have been cited as making a difference in a dating couple's ability to ignore stares and/or harassment.

A review of what literature exists on interracial unions involving couples of other racial combinations suggests that these relationships, too, are subject to tension and pressure (Spickard, 1989). Interracial unions in general draw societal concern because they encapsulate all of our unresolved feelings about race. Because we are a racially stratified society, in which races are viewed as being inherently separate, interactions among and between the races have always been viewed as problematic (Spickard, 1992). Interracial couples of all combinations face direct and indirect challenges inherent in concerns related to the maintenance of racial and ethnic classifications and identifications, social hierarchies, and cultural group values and norms (Azoulay, 1997; Comas-Diaz, 1996; Eschbach, 1995; Oriti, Bibb, &

Mahboubi, 1996; Stephan & Stephan, 1989, 1991). Such concerns are prevalent in relationships between Whites and Blacks, and many are even more prevalent in intermarriages involving Asians, Arabs, Latinos, and Native Americans.

According to Saenz, Hwang, Aguirre, and Anderson (1995), intermarriage represents one of the most accurate indicators of the assimilation process. In fact, the level of assimilation and acculturation appears to determine the extent to which individuals of immigrant groups are likely to intermarry. Insufficient data exists on Hispanic/Latino intermarriage (Thornton & Wason, 1995), but according to Comas-Diaz (1996), the Latino/Hispanic population embraces a rich tapestry of races and ethnicities, suggesting that this group has for a long time engaged in interracial unions. Macpherson and Stewart (1992) have indicated that foreign-born Hispanics or Latinos are more likely to marry outside of their groups than their native countrymen. The degree of intermarriage involving Japanese Americans may be related to generational issues and level of assimilation into the dominant culture (Spickard, 1989; Stephan & Stephan, 1989; Tinker, 1982). Similarly, among Chinese, the prevalence of intermarriage, especially with Whites, is related to the level of acculturation, facility with the English language, residential proximity, and socioeconomic status (Wong, 1989). Lee (1996), in discussing interracial marriages involving Asian Americans, indicated that although some interracial families appear able to integrate both cultures with a high degree of success, others often experience conflicts related to differences in values, religious beliefs, communication style, child rearing, and in-law influences. This may be due to issues of acculturation and assimilation.

The rate of intermarriage among Native Americans has continued to increase, particularly as Native American populations become more urbanized (Eschbach, 1995; Sandefur & McKinnell, 1986; Snipp, 1997). Another factor that has contributed to the increase in intermarriage among Native Americans is the erosion of racial boundaries and the lessening of conflicting attitudes of non-Natives toward American Indians (Snipp, 1997). According to Snipp (1997), there is a large amount of debate about whether American Indians ever received the same measure of scorn given to the African American population. If Native Americans have in fact experienced less prejudicial treatment, then the potential for their easier integration has been greater. Among Native Americans, level of acculturation and degree of closeness with one's reservation roots was indicated as having a great impact on issues of adjustment in interracial marriage (Attneave, 1982).

Intermarriage rates among Jewish individuals also seem to show an increase with increases in levels of acculturation and assimilation. Hence, among third-generation Jews, there has been a dramatic increase in out-marriage, including marriages across racial lines (Spickard, 1989).

Intermarriage between persons of color and European Americans has its share of cultural difficulties, but the challenges may be even more cumbersome when both intermarried partners are persons of color (Blau, 1998). For example, a Hispanic male–Chinese female interracial couple who appeared in an article on multiracial families in the December/January 1998 edition of *Child Magazine* talked about her family's reactions when they first met her spouse. They recalled that her family was taken aback by his physical appearance. This response was related to her parents' stereotypical attitudes and beliefs that men with facial hair were engaged in gang-like activities.

The cultural differences between interracial partners often present interesting dynamics and issues (Blau, 1998). Many of the issues related to cultural differences and conflicts are apparent at the start of the couple's relationship. Downey (1996), in discussing his experiences in an interracial relationship, talked about how he—a European American, Jewish male—had problems and conflicts related to cultural values and worldview differences regarding dating and relationships, which became apparent during his courtship with his Vietnamese wife. Their cultural differences resulted in a lack of support and acceptance from her family, which made the initial phases of their relationship a real challenge. Seeing their daughter's conflict about her commitment to this relationship and her commitment to them and her culture, her family finally relaxed. However, numerous concessions were made by all and involved Downey's own willingness to respect, learn more about, and adapt to the Vietnamese culture. Downey and his wife were able to come to a compromise. Their wedding was a blend of both of their backgrounds, which made them and their families happy and supportive.

The research I conducted with Dr. Jo Cohen yields interesting results and implications. Our study was a comprehensive qualitative investigation of the lives of over 80 Black-White married couples ranging in the number of years married from 1 year to 35 years. The couples came from various states along the Northeast Corridor and participated in extensive interviews that were conducted in their homes. The interview questions explored aspects of the couples' lives, including nuclear family background, dating history, courtship experiences, wedding, social life, public life, living and community environment, parenting and child-rearing experiences, education and employment experiences, values, and areas of stress and disagreement. The final sections of the interview explored issues regarding marital adjustment, communication, and decision making. Couples also responded to questions regarding experiences with counselors and their expectations of the counseling profession. The sample consisted largely of couples who were highly educated, professionally employed, and of middle class backgrounds. Hence, although the findings may not be generalizable to all interracial couples, they suggest some patterns and themes that have appeared significant. The lives of all of these couples are very similar to the lives of same-race couples as depicted in popular, contemporary media and literature.

The interracial partners of our research sample and the couples interviewed for this book describe their attractions to each other in ways parallel to partners of the same racial or ethnic background. These couples indicate such things as mutual interests, shared values and beliefs, ease in being in each other's company, and physical attractiveness. This is true in my own case. My husband and I were reared differently in some ways. I was an only child, raised by a single parent during my early formative years, until my mother remarried. I lived in the city of Philadelphia in a lower middle to middle class household. I was raised Catholic, my mother taught in the Catholic school system, and I attended Catholic schools until I went to college. My spouse was raised in a two-parent, middle class household. His family moved quite a bit because of his father's employment, but they typically lived in the suburbs. Although they were Catholic, my husband and his brother attended public schools. Despite these differences, we found ourselves able to relate to each other quite easily. We held common viewpoints on relationships, politics, education, and religion, to name a few. Our basic values are similar. Although we also found each other physically appealing, it was more the ease and comfort we had in being in each other's company that drew us together.

In *The Accidental Asian,* Eric Liu (1998) attempts to explain why he married a White woman. "It wasn't as if I had a plan. I wasn't trying to prove a point or defy convention. It was simply a matter of who was there and what was possible" (Liu, 1998, p. 182). He later says, "I chose to enter into a relationship with Carroll. Not with a 'White woman'. . . . Nobody—and nobody's subconscious—tricked me into falling in love with her" (p. 183).

The spouses in our sample reported sharing many common values and beliefs. The most common shared values were respect, honesty, trust, faithfulness, appreciation of diversity, family (including family of origin), and religion or spirituality. Expanding on this, one couple talked about the fact that their mutual values attracted them to each other and that at times it seemed that they had grown up in the same family and had been taught the same things. They attributed their marital success to these shared values. A Latin American woman and her White husband, as well as a Japanese woman and her Black husband, discussed how their shared values and beliefs reduced the level of potential conflict between them. Both couples felt that their shared values were particularly helpful to them when it came to maintaining consistency in their roles as parents.

The areas of greatest stress or tension for the couples in our research sample were reported as finances, juggling roles and responsibilities, parenting, employment (including number of hours spent at work and dual career issues), sexual relationship (involving the limited amount of attention given to intimacy and sexual relationship due to work, children, and daily pressures), communication related to dynamics of the relationship, and decision making issues. The couples who shared their experiences for purposes of this chapter expressed similar stressors and tensions. In their responses to questions concerning the impact of their racial or ethnic differences on their relationships, both groups of couples emphasized the fact that gender role differences, and, in some cases, religious differences, presented greater hurdles to overcome than their racial or ethnic differences.

For example, relationships involving European Americans of Jewish heritage who have interracially married present issues related to the influences of religious norms and beliefs (Azoulay, 1997). Often, it seems that religious differences are linked to and associated with individual partners' cultural backgrounds. David Mamet (1989) indicated that, like his parents, many Reform Jews look upon themselves as "racially" but not "religiously" Jewish. To be racially Jewish "meant that, among ourselves, we shared the wonderful, the warm, and the comforting codes, language, jokes, and attitudes which make up the consolations of strangers in a strange land."

The Latino American and Filipino American women I spoke with discussed their Catholic backgrounds as contributing strongly to their cultural upbringing and beliefs, including their beliefs regarding gender role responsibilities, children, and parenting. Asian and Indian women, particularly those of Hindu backgrounds, shared similar information relative to the link between the Hindu religion and their cultural backgrounds and beliefs. Here again, beliefs about role responsibilities, children, and parenting figure prominently, as do beliefs regarding the eating of red meat and pork.

Couples in both groups discussed the fact that in the everyday context of their relationships, their racial or ethnic differences did not present issues for them. The couples reported that their racial or ethnic differences become an issue only when they present themselves to the larger society where people see the contrasts in what they look like and react based on the differences that they see in skin color. According to Liu (1998), it is tempting to read every mixed coupling as a text on sexual politics, on the relative worth of skin hues, on the hidden insecurities of one spouse or another. To some people, the idea that love is more than skin deep sounds suspiciously like a pretext. To some people there must always be an ulterior motive. Another issue that emerged as a result of our discussions with Black-White interracial couples was the concern that people in the larger society have the perception and expectation that partners in interracial marriages argue or have conflicts with each other that are about their racial differences. These couples reported that their arguments and conflicts have nothing to do with their racial backgrounds.

One couple talked about an experience with a counselor who found it difficult to imagine that their racial differences did not create conflict in their relationship. The counselor further presented the couple with some assumptions that Black-White couples of lower socioeconomic backgrounds had a particularly difficult time because of social class issues. Similarly, other couples who participated in counseling reported that the counselor made judgments about the relationship based solely on the couple's racial differences, implying that the partners' different racial backgrounds contributed to their relational difficulties. In essence, the implication of these responses suggests that society, including counseling professionals, tends to make assumptions about these couples and their lives based on their appearance. For the couples, as discussed earlier, the fact that they are of different racial backgrounds has far less significance for them than it appears to have for society.

Interestingly, many of the couples of both groups shared views that suggest that they, too, may be influenced by the tainted perceptions of our society. For example, themes that emerged in comments made by a few White males married to non-Black women of color were feelings that Black-White couples had more difficulties than the speakers ever expected to have. Several White males married to Asian American women talked about experiencing greater difficulties than Black-White couples because of the cultural background differences between them and their Asian spouses. A theme that emerged in further discussion of this issue was a perception that most Black-White partners have grown up in and experienced American culture. This implies and suggests that depending on length of time in this country, as well as the level of acculturation and assimilation, the cultural values and worldviews of Asian Americans and European Americans may be dramatically different and hence may have an impact on the dynamics of the marriage. For immigrant and first-generation Asians and Hispanics, conflicts and differences related to communication patterns, language, gender roles, parenting styles and customs, and food were manifestations of profound cultural values and worldview differences. These differences and the differences that may exist between Blacks and Whites are legitimate and may be of valid concern, but these couples appeared willing and able to rise above the differences. As illustrated by Downey (1996) in discussing his experience with his Vietnamese wife, unwillingness of one or both partners to respect and learn about the other's cultural background, including rituals, customs, and traditions, can have far-reaching implications in the relationship between the partners and in the relationship they both have with the families of origin, in-laws, friends, and associates. The notion of child rearing presents even bigger issues in this regard.

Issues of Parenting and Child Rearing

Multiracial couples also discuss questions related to where to live and whether or not to have children. However, these concerns and the question regarding how to raise their children have different meanings for these couples. In fact, child rearing and parenting are the most important and complicated issues interracial couples face, with the major concern being how their children will be accepted and viewed by society (Blau, 1998). According to Wardle (1992a), because interracial marriage has been taboo in this country for so long, there are many myths about these marriages as well as the children of these unions. Among these are suggestions that offspring of interracial marriage have more social and psychological problems than do other children (Gibbs, 1987). Modern-day interracial couples are challenged to deal with these societal pressures while at the same time raising their children with a pride and healthy self-esteem in their dual heritages (Brandell, 1988).

The issue most often disputed concerning biracial children is their racial identity (Melina, 1990). Concerns regarding racial identity typically begin with questions related to the child's physical characteristics. Even before birth, questions are raised relative to the child's phenotype. Numerous couples in the sample for the research conducted by Kenney and Cohen (1998) discussed the fact that prior to the births of their children, questions were raised, even by strangers, regarding how their children might look. A Filipino American woman and her Swiss-German husband discussed the shocked reactions of both of their families to the appearance of their son. The reaction seemed linked to each family's desire to claim the child as a part of themselves. Assumptions are made suggesting that the biracial child is genetically more one race than the other (Wardle, 1992a).

Parents interviewed by Kenney and Cohen, as well as parents interviewed for this chapter, discussed situations in which one or the other parent had been asked questions regarding his or her parentage because of the child's physical appearance. Again, some of these questions had been posed by strangers. For example, one day as I sat in a public powder-room holding our first daughter after nursing her, an older White woman entered the room, made a comment about how beautiful she was, and then asked if I was her nurse. My daughter was very fair skinned, with straight black hair. Being that I was of a different generation and time, and feeling caught a little off guard, I was not entirely sure what the woman meant. My sister-in-law, who entered the room right after the woman, immediately responded, "No, she's the child's mother" and then clarified for me that the woman thought that I was the "wet nurse." I recall that my anger and hurt around this experience focused on the question of my parentage. I wondered if this would be a constant experience for me and for my child.

Another Black woman, married to a White man, who also participated in our study reported a similar experience. She and her fair-skinned, blonde-haired daughter were shopping in a clothing store. Her daughter, who was three at the time, began to misbehave, and the mother, in turn, began to chastise her in the middle of an aisle. To her dismay and outrage, an older White woman approached her and began yelling at her for what she assumed was mistreatment of a child that couldn't possibly be hers because she was Black and the child looked White.

Similarly, a European American father of two biracial (Chinese-European American) children recalled numerous occasions when he was out alone with his children. People made the assumption that his children were adopted because of their Asian features. A Mayan male and his German-heritage wife also described stares of curiosity from people who see him (described as dark skinned) out alone with his fair-skinned son. Corin Ramos (1997) summarized this type of experience in an article written for *Interrace Magazine* when she disclosed, "I have an unreasonable fear of being mistaken for my daughters' nanny. What if they grow up embarrassed or ashamed of me?" (p. 16). This question posed by Ramos, a Filipino woman married to a White man, is one that many interracial parents, including myself and my spouse, have asked.

Many parents insist that their children have an identity based on the collective backgrounds of both parents (Brandell, 1988; McRoy & Freeman, 1986; Wardle, 1987). They raise their children to embrace and celebrate both cultures equally and therefore expose their children to the values, roles, norms, attitudes, behaviors, and, perhaps, the language of both cultures (Stephan & Stephan, 1991). The majority of the couples we interviewed spoke of wanting their children to have a sense of and appreciation for all of their cultural backgrounds and heritages. Many of them gave examples of how, beginning very early in their children's lives, they attempted to introduce them to the various aspects of their backgrounds. Others raised their children to identify exclusively with one ethnic group. The couples interviewed who adopted this process provided a rationale for their decision based on their children's physical appearance and how society would view them. For example, some Black-White couples and Asian-White couples whose children had physical features that were prominently African or Asian felt that it was easier for the child to be identified as such. However, among couples who were Asian and Black or Latino and Asian, there appeared to be a pattern toward rearing children with an identification and appreciation of both cultures. Whatever the choice, it is important that parents be comfortable about their decisions and instill a sense of comfort in their children (Tucker, 1996). Liu (1998) indicates that he cannot imagine requiring his children to be very Chinese or not at all Chinese. He intends to give his children the choice, but first, he will give them the ability to know why they choose.

> They will learn how their family came to be, from what corners of the world their ancestors sprang, what tongues and rituals once flourished under their names. They will be exposed to their inheritance—even, I hope, that part of the inheritance I have let fall into disuse. And they will decide. (p. 197)

Interracial relationships involving White and non-White parents in particular have the challenge of helping their children cope with racism. This may come in the form of racial jokes and slurs, acts of discrimination, or outright rejection. There may even be rejection on the part of relatives and family members (Rosenblatt, Karis, & Powell, 1995; Stephan & Stephan, 1991). A Black man and his White wife who were married in the late 1950s shared with us the pain that they and later their children experienced because her parents had disowned her upon learning of her intentions to marry a Black man. She continues to experience the pain of this rejection. Her parents both died, leaving her without a chance to bring closure to the relationship and her children without an opportunity to know their maternal grandparents.

A Korean female and White male with two children discussed the extent to which they candidly share with their young children some of the racial slurs and comments they may hear when out in public or at school. They reported how they have even at times referred to the children using some stereotypical terminology, feeling that if they hear this at home, it will not come as a shock or surprise when they hear it from others. This may appear somewhat extreme, but these parents feel as though they are preparing their children for the cruelty of the world.

A multiracial woman of Asian-Indian and English background who grew up in North Dakota recommends that parents of multiracial children be vigilant in paying close attention to how their children are faring in social interactions with peers. Her father, a dark-skinned Asian-Indian man, and her mother, a blonde-haired, fair-skinned woman born and raised in England, moved to North Dakota when the subject and her sister were of preschool age and before her brother was born. The children, who describe themselves as the ones with the darkest hair and skin of any of their schoolmates, experienced considerable harassment from their blond-haired, fair-skinned peers. As adults, they are looked at with great curiosity whenever they return home for a visit. The issues presented by their difference were not addressed with them by their parents until they reached adulthood. Hence, they were each forced to develop coping skills for dealing with the harassment on their own.

Parents in the research sample on Black-White marriages conducted by Rosenblatt et al. (1995) discussed the steps they took to help their children reach adulthood without being drastically hurt by racism. They emphasized the importance of talking with their children about issues of identity; providing strong options for support from extended family, play family, and friends; and providing identity-bolstering books, toys, and films. In addition, they spoke of the significance of providing strong adult role models for their children, building good connections to a strong Black community, and providing instruction for their children about what to say and how to respond in various situations (Rosenblatt et al., 1995).

Similar implications can be drawn from the results of research conducted by Stephan and Stephan (1989, 1991) on or about mixed-heritage Japanese Americans and Hispanics. Several Hispanic partners who were interviewed for this chapter indicated the significance of maintaining close familial ties and ties to the Hispanic community. They cited the necessity of their children's learning to speak Spanish, being a part of cultural activities, and enjoying customary foods as being of particular importance. According to Mamet (1989), Jewish food and Jewish jokes are a significant aspect in the maintenance of Jewish "culture" as well.

As children become of school age and their involvement with peers and the larger society increases, the aforementioned concerns, particularly identity-related concerns, intensify. Parents of younger school-age children, especially, express concerns related to the level of sensitivity and support provided to children of mixed heritage in the school setting by administrators and teachers, as well as by their peers (Wardle, 1991, 1992a). Of special interest to many parents is the extent to which the school setting offers diversity, multicultural sensitivity, and a multicultural environment and curriculum. In this matter, the home location, the school district, and the diversity offered become significant for many couples (Kenney, Kenney, & Cohen, 1994).

Children of mixed heritage living in diverse environments are likely to adjust more easily with respect to their ethnic identity, as they are likely to face less pressure to conform to rigid ethnic identities. In essence, a more diverse community is likely to accommodate the existence of multiethnic identities (Saenz et al., 1995). A Korean American woman and her White husband who live in a rural setting of Pennsylvania articulated some concerns around these issues. As a resolution to their concerns, they decided to send their children to a school located within her sister's more diverse suburban community. Similarly, a White woman and her Black husband made the decision to move to a more diverse community and enroll their daughter in the school district there because of the discrimination their daughter experienced in their previous all-White community, beginning at the age of 4 years, and because of the lack of diversity of the school district in rural Birdsboro, Pennsylvania, where they previously lived.

Gay and Lesbian
Interracial Couples

There has also been an increase in the rates of interracial coupling among gay and lesbian couples. Research and literature on these relationships is very limited, but there is evidence that suggests that more of these relationships involve Black gay men, which further suggests that there may be factors involved in these relationships similar to those in interracial relationships involving Black heterosexual males. Factors related to the social community, such as the extent to which the community is perceived as being liberal, tolerant, and open minded, thereby offering opportunities for meeting partners of other races, are significant (Peplau, Cochran, & Mays, 1997). In addition, however, interracial relationships among Black gay males may be related to limited partner choice (Mays, Cochran, & Rhue, 1993). In the African American community, where homosexual relationships are stigmatized, finding a Black partner may be difficult (Cochran & Mays, 1988a, 1988b; Mays et al., 1993). The potential of being "outed" creates feelings of vulnerability (Adams & Kimmel, 1997). Hence, issues of physical and social proximity to persons of other races figure greatly for these males (Parks & Eggert, 1993). It is possible that these issues are prevalent for Asian and Latino gays and lesbians as well (Chan, 1992; Morales, 1992). Lesbians of color, particularly Black lesbians, engage in relationships with women who are not from their same ethnic groups more frequently than White lesbians (Mays & Cochran, 1988a, 1988b; Tafoya & Rowell, 1988).

Several authors, in discussion of the concerns of gays and lesbians of Asian, Latino, and African American backgrounds, have alluded to the complexities that may surround the relationships of persons in these groups, especially interracial relationships with White Americans (Chan, 1992; Greene & Boyd-Franklin, 1996; Gutierrez & Dworkin, 1992; Morales, 1992). The major issues for these couples include the acceptance of the gay or lesbian individual's sexual preference by the individual of color's family and cultural community (Chan, 1992; Gutierrez & Dworkin, 1992; Morales, 1992) and the acceptance of the interracial relationship by family and community (Greene, 1994a, 1994b; Greene & Boyd-Franklin, 1996; Gutierrez & Dworkin, 1992; Pearlman, 1996). Of salient concern here is the extent to which the partner of color not only experiences acceptance from the cultural community but feels supported by the White partner for his or her efforts to maintain connectedness to the culture and cultural community (Greene, 1994a, 1994b; Greene & Boyd-Franklin, 1996; Gutierrez & Dworkin, 1992; Pearlman, 1996).

As racism and bigotry is just as prevalent in the gay and lesbian communities as it is outside them, the extent to which the person of color feels comfortable navigating within the gay and lesbian community becomes significant as well. As a result of racism, as well as classism, some interracial couples choose not to affiliate with the gay and lesbian community. This is particularly true for those who live in communities that lack diversity (Johnson & Keren, 1996). Lesbians of color often wear a protective psychological armor and develop defensive coping strategies for dealing with racism (Sears, 1987). Black lesbians often experience feelings of resentment and jealousy toward their White partners for their privileged status (Clunis & Green, 1988; Greene, 1994a). In the case of men involved in interracial relationships, Johnson and Keren (1996) indicate that they often find themselves negotiating differing notions of power and privilege, expectations about visibility, and expectations of where and how support for the relationship will be sought.

The extent to which the person of color feels supported and validated in his or her experiences by the White partner is important (Gutierrez & Dworkin, 1992; Pearlman, 1996). In a relationship with a lesbian of color, for example, a White lesbian may encounter racism for the first time. How the White partner deals with it often affects the relationship (Clunis & Green, 1988). A White partner who is naive about comments that are racist in origin may experience her partner's anger as inappropriate. The White partner may overreact and criticize her partner for being complacent in her response to situations that are racist in nature. She may also be presumptuous or patronizing and assume the role of rescuer, a role that her partner may not want or need (Greene, 1994a). Other reactions White lesbian partners have exhibited that manifest in the relationship are feelings of guilt about White racism and political hypervigilance (Clunis & Green, 1988). Additionally, both partners in the interracial relationship may have to deal with shaming questions regarding their individual loyalties to their own cultural group (Clunis & Green, 1988; Greene, 1994a).

Gay and lesbian interracial couples who have shared their experiences for purposes of this chapter have validated much of the above written information. The complexities inherent in society's stigmatized views of gays and lesbians, as well as persons of color, add a level of stress to these relationships that appears greater than that experienced by heterosexual interracial couples, including Black-White heterosexual couples. One Black-White heterosexual couple we interviewed described a conversation the partners had with a member of the White partner's family early in their relationship, in which the family member indicated relief on learning that his sibling at least was not in a lesbian relationship.

The literature on African American lesbians involved in interracial relationships with European American lesbians suggests that although racial and cultural differences present concerns for the relationships, they are not the source of all problems experienced by the couple. Couples, however, will at times overemphasize their visible differences and the influence that these differences have on their problems. Although, surely, racial differences can be the cause of significant concerns, other concerns resulting from individual intrapsychic issues and dynamics may be experienced as being inherent in the couple's racial or cultural differences (Greene & Boyd-Franklin, 1996).

The Significance and Insignificance of
Racial Differences for Interracial Couples

As in the case of Mildred Jeters and Richard Loving (see Chapter 1), most interracial couples that were interviewed married because of their love for each other. When one examines the significance of the issue of race for these couples, it appears that it is not that they are denying their racial differences and the significance and impact that race has come to have in this country, it is perhaps that they view and deal with these differences in a different context. Although this context may appear to some to minimize the importance of racial differences in the day-to-day aspects and dynamics of the relationship, it does not invalidate the significance that is placed on racial differences in the larger social schema by way of the racial oppression and discrimination felt by partners of color who are in these relationships as they navigate in society.

The couples from both groups who had been married for over 20 or 30 years reported that from a racial difference standpoint, the societal pressures they experienced were much stronger than those experienced by younger couples. This validates the reports in the literature that cited interracial couples of the 1960s and 1970s facing pressures not only with regard to family rejection and social alienation but to matters including lack of acceptance by places of recreation and employment and difficulties finding suitable housing in certain neighborhoods and communities (Cretser & Leon, 1982; Porterfield, 1978, 1982). Many of the older couples expressed the opinion that the Civil Rights Movement, the Loving Decision, and the growth in the number of couples dating and marrying interracially have helped to improve things for the multiracial population in general. In spite of the strong pressures, these couples felt that the strength and security each partner had within him- or herself and within the relationship helped them and their children survive. They also felt that the racial differences that existed between them were more of an issue for others. The areas of greatest stress and tension within the marriage were concerns that appear typical to most marriages. Marital conflicts and arguments had nothing to do with racial differences.

Two issues emerged that may be helpful to explore, particularly in interracial relationships involving Whites and persons of color. The first issue concerns where each partner is in terms of his or her own racial identity development. The second issue concerns where each partner is in terms of his or her acknowledgment and acceptance of the existence of racism and the role that racism plays in his or her life. Walt Harrington (1992), in writing the book *Crossings: A White Man's Journey Into Black America,* tells of an experience he had while in a dentist's chair, when a visiting dentist told a racist joke, unaware of the fact that Harrington's wife is Black and his children "tan" and "bright tan." The experience resulted in his recognition and acknowledgment of having "crossed a line."

For an instant I've traveled to a place where White Americans rarely go. I feel revulsion and anger at this man. I feel fear and anguish for my children. I feel hopeless. Am I, I wonder, feeling like a Black male? (pp. 1-2)

Harrington's (1992) response to this experience and the similar responses of other White partners and parents to situations such as this resulted in my efforts to explore a concept that I refer to as "racial/cultural empathy." My husband's response to the incident I reported experiencing in the ladies room was one of shock at the absurdity of the woman's statement. He later verbalized having feelings of anger toward the woman because her comment was hurtful to him as well as to me.

The achievement of racial/cultural empathy occurs via a developmental process, which I feel White partners of interracial relationships experience as they grow through their relationships. An additional part of the exploration for the White partner also involves acknowledging and accepting "White privilege" and the role it has had in his or her own life. Not all White partners who people of color choose are able to journey across the country exploring these issues as Walt Harrington did. However, it is the manner in which the White partners respond to the exploration and the impact that such exploration has upon their behavior in a social context with the larger racial, ethnic, and political communities that matters for the individual, the partner of color, and the relationship (Frankenberg, 1995). The solidarity and success of many of the relationships of the couples involved in the groups I have identified in this chapter is a manifestation of the extent to which the partners (particularly the White partners) have addressed and explored all of these issues in relation to themselves individually, in the context of the relationship, and in relation to the children they may be raising.

Implications for Counseling
Interracial Couples

As indicated in Chapter 1, the counseling profession has only recently begun to address the issues and concerns of the multiracial population. Counselors have had limited experience working with interracial couples and have often relied on dated literature that depicts interracial relationships as being fraught with pathology and doomed to failure. As mentioned earlier in this chapter, some couples have reported working with counselors who made judgments about their relationship problems based on the partners' racial differences. These judgments were based on assumptions that racial or cultural background differences result in relational difficulties. McGoldrick, Giordano, and Pearce (1996) suggest that the greater the cultural difference between spouses, the more problems they have adjusting to marriage. I have not found this to be the case and urge counselors to be careful about making this assumption.

With the increase in interracial partnerships and marriages, counselors may find themselves working with an increased number of interracial couples. Several factors are important when counseling these couples. First, the counselor must be aware of the biases and assumptions that he or she may have with respect to interracial couples and interracial unions. The counselor must also be willing to gain knowledge and understanding of each partner and the cultural values and worldview that each partner brings to the relationship. Each partner's worldview will have an impact on the relationship, and it is crucial that the counseling professional be aware of this impact and how it is manifested in the partners' interactions with one another, as well as with others.

The counselor must also assess the extent to which each partner understands and accepts the cultural values and worldview of the other. In cases where this understanding is lacking, the counselor will need to assist each person in understanding the significant impact that one's cultural values and beliefs have on individual feelings and behaviors and, subsequently, on the dynamics and conflicts of the relationship (Ibrahim & Schroeder, 1990). The purpose of this assessment and exploratory process is to assist the partners in a couple in understanding each other as cultural beings and why culture is significant to the dynamics of the relationship. The assessment is also meant to help each partner understand how changes in individual cultural precepts can negatively affect individual self-concept and may not be realistic or desirable for a partner. Hence, requiring the partners to come to an acceptance of each other and of each other's culture makes it possible for them to be able to make mutual compromises and changes (Ibrahim & Schroeder, 1990).

The counselor must be willing to learn and use strategies and skills that are culturally appropriate for each partner, keeping in mind the need to help the couple understand that its partners' different cultural frameworks may dictate the use of different approaches when the counselor is working with each of them. Ultimately, the counselor must be open to working with the couple around the issues and needs the partners present, not around what the counselor assumes the problems to be. Chapter 5 will provide a more extensive presentation of treatment, as well as intervention strategies to consider when working with this population.

Summary

This chapter began with a discussion of the lives of contemporary interracial couples. A discussion of issues of parenting and child rearing followed, including salient social and cultural issues associated with the raising of multiracial children. Next, the chapter addressed the issues and concerns of gay and lesbian interracial couples. Reports of research conducted on the lives of interracial couples, regardless of sexual orientation, was included throughout the chapter. The majority of the research findings reported were from research with Black-White interracial married couples, but a sample of couples of other interracial blends (as well as gay and lesbian couples) provided information on their experiences. The chapter ended with a discussion of the significance and insignificance of racial difference in the lives of interracial couples. A tenet this author has developed, racial/cultural empathy, was introduced, and implications for counseling interracial couples were explored.

3

Multiracial Individuals

Issues Across the Lifespan

In an effort to help monoracial people of the United States understand the currently burgeoning multiracial population, the popular press has given much publicity to issues and strengths of people of mixed race heritage (e.g., Aubrey, 1995; Beech, 1996; Blau, 1998; Cose, 1995; Courtney, 1995; Funderberg, 1994; Leland & Beals, 1997; Morganthau, 1995; Peterson, 1997a, 1997b; von Sternberg, 1995a, 1995b). The helping services professional literature has lagged behind the popular press in recognizing multiracial people. Counselor education and counseling psychology programs are beginning to include this population as one with which their graduate students will be working in increasing numbers. There is a gradual expansion of the professional literature to address counseling and psychological services for multiracial people and interracial couples.

One of the purposes of this chapter is to explore the salient issues of multiracial individuals across the lifespan, from childhood through adulthood. Because many of these issues are related to racial reference group identity, models of racial identity development are also examined and limitations of early models of racial identity development delineated. Information from recent studies of biracial and multiracial identity development is presented, and some implications for the process of counseling with multiracial individuals and families are introduced.

Issues of Multiracial Individuals

Myths and stereotypes about multiracial people and about couples in interracial relationships still cloud the perspectives that some people have of individuals with more than one racial heritage. These myths and stereotypes remain as issues that multiracial people face. One of the most damaging of these myths is the "one drop" rule described in the first chapter of this book. Wehrly's (1996) book *Counseling Interracial Individuals and Families* details other myths and stereotypes and states that "there is a great need for society to move beyond these pervasive myths and stereotypes and to see interracial people and people of color as full partners in the human race" (p. 10).

The multiracial individual whose physical appearance does not indicate that he or she is a member of one of the sociopolitically defined single racial groups challenges conventional racial ideology. "In highly racialized U.S. society, one's assignment into a sociopolitically defined single racial group is necessary in order to be a socially recognized, functional member of the society" (Williams, 1996, p. 193). U.S. society operates primarily on a monoracial model of race relations and racial identity development that does not allow for variations in physical appearance (Root, 1997a, 1997b).

As a result, multiracial individuals constantly face questions as to who or what they are (Houston, 1997; Ramirez, 1996; Wiggins, 1998; Williams, 1996). Associated with these neverending queries may come feelings that they are unique or do not belong. These issues of identity surface as soon as multiracial children are old enough to recognize that they are different and may persist as long as they live (Bradshaw, 1992; Williams, 1996). At an early age, multiracial children begin to learn the process of relating to people from different groups.

Issues that bring multiracial clients to counseling, however, may not always be related to their multiracial heritages (Gibbs, 1987, 1989; McRoy & Freeman, 1986; Wehrly, 1996). Because the age and development of each multiracial person can influence the way that person deals with having more than one racial heritage, issues of multiracial individuals will be discussed from a developmental perspective.

Issues of Multiracial Children

Houston (1997) describes children of interracial and international Asian marriages as unique children "between two cultures [who] embrace the joys of those worlds and are challenged by the heartaches" (p. 154). Page (1996) pictures biracial children as "quite special people with special needs in a society more obsessed with race than its members usually care to admit [and living] on the margins of America's historical racial contradictions" (p. 284). He recognizes, however, that times are changing and that "a new generation of post-1960s multiracial children is demanding recognition, not in the margins of society but as a mainstream of their very own" (p. 284).

Through overt questions such as "What are you?" or "Who are you?" and covert communications such as quizzical staring, multiracial children learn that they do not "fit" traditional patterns of racial identification. At first, children with more than one racial heritage may be flattered by this attention, but being the objects of ongoing curiosity can result in their interpreting this difference as bad and blaming themselves for being different (Root, 1990).

Some multiracial children recognize the negative implications of the question the first time they hear it. One of the participants in our research, Carmen Salazar Lowhar (whose Panamanian father is of Spanish, Italian, Basque, and South American Indian heritage and whose mother was of Euro-American English descent), writes:

> I vividly remember a day on the playground when a white girl shouted at me. . . . "What are you, Mexican or something?" I remember feeling such an outrage at her question and assumption that I was Mexican, because I knew that to be Mexican in southern California was equal to being considered pretty low. And besides, couldn't she see I was white? I instantly tried to distance myself from being considered Mexican. I shouted back to her that "No, I'm not Mexican!" but didn't explain what I was probably because I had never conceptualized what I was. (Personal communication, April 8, 1998)

Societal racism compounds the successful attainment of normal developmental tasks for multiracial children who frequently encounter racism. The ambiguity of their racial status can add vulnerabilities not faced by children with monoracial identity (Brandell, 1988; Herring, 1995). Being on the receiving end of name calling and teasing are common experiences for mixed-race children (Blau, 1998; Houston, 1997). Multiracial young people with dark skin may be called "nigger," "peanut butter," "jig-a-boo," or "monkey." Other derogatory names include "slant eyes," "Chink," "Mexican," "spic," "wetback," or "half breed."

It has long been recognized that most parents receive little or no training for one of the most important jobs of their life, that of being a parent. The task of parenting can be especially challenging for parents whose racial heritages are different because they may have had no parental models to emulate in their attempts to raise biracial or multiracial children. The daughter of a Puerto Rican and Venezuelan father and a mother of German, English, and Swiss descent told about the way her parents tried to teach their multiracial children to ignore name calling and teasing:

> My parents taught my three sisters, brother, and me to accept we were different in others' eyes, but within, God made us all the same. "We all bleed the same color," my father would say! We were to let everything roll off our backs and be proud of whom we were. Still, it was very difficult. (Anna M. Barbosa, personal communication, March 9, 1998)

Development of a unified and positive identity with all aspects of their racial heritages can be confusing and challenging for multiracial children. In an interview for *Teaching Tolerance* magazine, Michael Dorris told how painful and schizophrenic it was to try to understand the behavior of some of his French, Modoc Indian, and Irish relatives (Aronson, 1995). Reddy (1994) describes the confusion that her preschool biracial son, Sean, experienced in trying to understand that racial characteristics are independent of gender and age characteristics.

The most significant issue faced by children with more than one racial heritage is the development of a positive multiracial identity. Some multiracial children face pressures to identify with only one of their racial heritages (Blau, 1998; Bowles, 1993; Funderburg, 1994; McRoy & Freeman, 1986; Rosenblatt, Karis, & Powell, 1995; Steel, 1995; Wardle, 1992a, 1993; Winn & Priest, 1993). When individuals identify with only one of their multiracial heritages, they do not integrate the other heritage(s) into their racial self-identity. Sooner or later these individuals will feel the loss of the missing part(s) of their identity and will suffer because of this loss. When multiracial children are not accepted by relatives of both their paternal and maternal heritages and when the family does not live in a multiracial community, the challenge to identify with all of their racial roots may be magnified. This is particularly true when the family lives in a community that is predominantly White and the children attend a school with very few children of color.

Many multiracial children are cherished by the families of both their mother and their father. Some, however, may experience rejection by one or both sides of the family (Houston, 1997; Root, 1995). Three recent autobiographical odysseys, *Divided to the Vein: A Journey into Race and Family* (Minerbrook, 1996), *The Color of Water: A Black Man's Tribute to His White Mother* (McBride, 1996), and *Life on the Color Line: The True Story of a White Boy Who Discovered He Was Black* (Williams, 1995) recount the painful experiences of multiracial Black-White children who were deprived of contacts with half of their racial heritages. Although most of the respondents to our interviews felt acceptance from both sides of their families, others were aware of a lack of support from relatives on one or both sides of the family.

Stresses in parental adjustment to an interracial marriage may place the children at risk for behavioral and emotional problems (Adler, 1987). When parents are caught up in their own issues, it is difficult for them to offer the nurturing that may be needed for the multiracial child to develop a positive self-concept (Brandell, 1988; McRoy & Freeman, 1986; Wardle, 1993).

Another issue arises in multiracial families when the skin color of siblings is different. Skin color differences seem to be particularly common in children of Black-White heritage. However, skin color differences may also be evident in children of other mixed race parentage. The importance of helping Black-White multiracial children deal with the meaning that skin color and physical features may have to other people is addressed by Rosenblatt et al. (1995).

Extended family members sometimes treat multiracial children differently based on the physical appearance of the children. The child with darker skin may be a target of racism; the light-skinned Black-White child with straight hair may be seen as White by the larger society. It can be tempting to pass as White, but passing "can bring with it a lifetime of identity struggles, the unpleasantness of secret keeping, and personal and family pain arising from efforts to hide the existence of relatives of color from certain people" (Rosenblatt et al., 1995, p. 211). Biracial Black-White children may face even more racism than the racism faced by Black children. In addition, biracial Black-White children may threaten White privilege by claiming property and power that historically were reserved for White people.

Reddy (1994) addresses institutional racism in schools and discusses how institutionalized racism is related to the unearned privileges that accompany White skin. School administrators, faculty, and staff are rarely aware of White privilege and ways in which they perpetuate institutionalized racism. Children can be cruel to those who are different and add stress to the lives of their multiracial peers. School personnel need training in cultural sensitivity and recognition of racism so that they will address prejudice and institutionalized racism in the school environment (Nishimura, 1995; Nishimura & Bol, 1997; Wehrly, 1996).

Multiracial children will also face racism in other aspects of their lives. Caring adults will not always be there to protect them. It appears that a developmental task of the multiracial child in contemporary society is to learn how to face racism (Houston, 1997; Lloyd, 1989; Root, 1998; Wehrly, 1996). Houston (1997) believes that parents of multiracial Asian children have the obligation to go beyond traditional parental responsibilities and act as societal change agents by serving as "windows of understanding to a stubborn monoracial society" (p. 154). Houston's recommendation might also apply to the parents of any multiracial children.

Parents of multiracial children recognize that their children have strengths not shared by children of monoracial heritage (Rosenblatt et al., 1995). At an early age, multiracial children learn to relate to and negotiate with people from at least two cultures. In so doing, they develop strengths and flexibilities that some monoracial people never acquire.

Children also recognize that growing up multiracial has strengths. In *Trevor's Story* (Kandel, 1997), 10-year-old Trevor tells how he is probably not as prejudiced as other kids and that he does not "make fun of people or judge them because of their differences" (p. 33). Trevor also believes that he has helped other kids to be more accepting and tolerant of differences and to realize that "It's what's on the inside that counts" (p. 33).

Issues of Multiracial Adolescents

In Western cultures, the period of adolescence is viewed as tumultuous because it is the time when young people experience the stress of establishing a unique identity that includes independence from families while conforming to peer group norms. It is normal for adolescents with a monoracial heritage to experience stress in their struggles to attain this unique identity. "Developing this stable, single identity with a dual- or multiracial heritage that reflects positive aspects of both (or all) heritages and rejects societal self-limiting stereotypes can be an even larger task" (Wehrly, 1996, p. 77).

For the young person with more than one racial heritage, adolescence can be extra stressful because identity issues become racial issues (Poussaint, 1984; Root, 1990). The multiracial adolescent may find that he or she is no longer welcome in certain friendship circles and that peers may be influenced by family members who object to cross-racial relationships (Root, 1990). A central issue related to renegotiating social relationships is that of answering two questions: "Who am I?" and "Where do I fit?" (Gibbs, 1987; Overmier, 1990).

Multiracial adolescents often feel that no one understands them, not even their parents (Nishimura, 1998; Root, 1990). They may also feel that they are the only ones in their school who have parents of different races (Jones,

1992), and they may be unaware of other students with mixed-race heritage at their school. Open discussions of racial identity or of racist incidents may not be a part of either their home or their school environments. Circumstances such as these can exacerbate feelings of differentness and loneliness (Wehrly, 1996).

The biracial interviewees in Funderburg's (1994) book *Black, White, Other* talked about the prejudice and racism they experienced as adolescents. One of the young women recalled having to defend both her Black side and her White side, although defending the White side did not start until high school. The young woman's parents had taught her how to show pride in both sides of her heritage, but she found it most difficult to deal with White peers who made racist generalizations and then said they didn't mean to include her when they made these statements.

Choosing a racial reference group identification involves critical decisions (Pinderhughes, 1995). Multiracial adolescents may experience peer (and sometimes parental) pressures to identify with only one of their racial heritages (Cauce et al., 1992; Kerwin, 1991; Kerwin & Ponterotto, 1995; Rosenblatt et al., 1995; Steel, 1995; Winn & Priest, 1993). Choosing to identify with one racial heritage and rejecting the other heritage(s) can cause the multiracial individual to feel disloyal and/or guilty (Sebring, 1985).

As with younger children in multiracial families, adolescents can be negatively affected when parents have neither resolved differences nor accepted each other's cultural heritage. The multiracial adolescent can be "drawn into the parental conflict and must either renounce one identity at the expense of the other, split his or her identity into two different camps, or live with the anxiety of identity diffusion" (Gibbs & Moskowitz-Sweet, 1991, p. 588).

Accounts of an excess of problems and issues among multiracial adolescents have come from studies of multiracial teens in psychological treatment (Gibbs, 1987, 1989). Results of these reports have led to the impression that all mixed-race young people have serious psychological problems and are marginally accepted by society.

Investigations of the mental health of multiracial youth *not* in psychological treatment have helped to dispel the earlier negative image of young people with more than one racial heritage. A study of the social adjustment of biracial African American-White and Asian-White youth (Cauce et al., 1992) compared a group of biracial early adolescents with a matched group of monoracial young people whose family heritage was the same as the biracial youths' parents of color. "Key analyses in these studies suggest that biracial adolescents were indistinguishable from adolescents of color who were similar to themselves . . . and clearly suggest that biracial adolescents can be healthy, competent, and well adjusted" (Cauce et al., 1992, pp. 218 & 221).

A 2-year study of the psychosocial adjustment of *nonclinical* Black-White adolescents by Gibbs and Hines (1992) found that three fourths of these biracial teens *not* in counseling were comfortable in negotiating positive aspects of both of their racial heritages, had developed satisfactory peer and social relationships, were managing sexual and aggressive impulses satisfactorily, had achieved a healthy separation from parents, and were establishing appropriate educational and career plans.

By gathering information on the ethnicity of both parents in large surveys of both ethnically diverse and predominantly White areas of Southern California, Phinney and Alipuria (1996) were able to gather normal samples of multiethnic high school and college students and compare them with their monoethnic peers. They found that the multiethnic young people were not disadvantaged psychologically. "A self-esteem measure did not indicate any difference in terms of psychological well-being between the multiethnic individuals and monoethnic peers in either study" (p. 152). An additional measure of attitudes toward other groups indicated that some of the multiethnic high school students had more positive attitudes toward other groups than did their monoethnic peers.

In a study of the identity development of Asian-White late adolescents, Grove (1991) found that young people of mixed Asian and White heritages had resolved racial issues so that race was not a daily source of contention. Other studies that present a picture of positive adjustment to their racial heritages by multiracial adolescents and young adults are those of Alipuria (1990), Field (1992, 1996), Kerwin (1991), and Tizard and Phoenix (1995).

Winn and Priest (1993) noted that each client has several self-identity factors and that multiracial adolescents may use several in self-descriptions. The identity factors chosen for self-description vary according to context and life stage. They cite an African American–Asian adolescent female who could "use her African-American identity, her Asian identity, her female identity, her adolescent identity, or any combination of these as a means of self-expression" (p. 34).

The cover story "For today's teens, race 'not an issue anymore' " (Peterson, 1997a) in the November 3, 1997 *USA Today* indicates that attitudes toward cross-racial dating are changing among teenagers. In the October 13 to 20, 1997 Gallup Poll survey reported in the *USA Today* cover story, 57% of the teenagers who had dated responded that they had been out with someone of a different race, either White, Black, Asian, or Hispanic. Thirty percent indicated that they had not dated cross racially but would consider it. Only 13% of the teenagers surveyed indicated that they would not consider cross-racial dating.

In a separate news story in the same issue of *USA Today,* "Interracial dating is no big deal for teens" (Peterson, 1997b), the young people talked about interracial dating and how they feel comfortable in these relationships in the school environment. Some admitted, however, that they did not feel that they had parental or societal approval for this behavior.

Issues of Multiracial Adults

In the past, development of a multiracial reference group identity has been viewed as a task of childhood and adolescence. We now know that many multiracial people continue the struggle to integrate dual or multiple racial heritages with other aspects of their identity throughout their lifetime (Nishimura, 1998; Root, 1998). Mixed-race adults, like mixed-race adolescents, often feel that no one, not even parents or close friends, really understands the unique situations they face or the intrapersonal conflict they experience (Root, 1990).

Mixed racial heritage does not in itself lead to psychological maladjustment. A majority of multiracial adults are psychologically well adjusted and comfortable with their dual heritages (Alipuria, 1990; Hall, 1980, 1992; Johnson & Nagoshi, 1986; Lloyd, 1989; Stephan & Stephan, 1989, 1991; Thornton, 1983). It is the internalized racist beliefs in the environment that can cause psychological distress (Adams, 1997; Root, 1994).

The problem of institutionalized racism noted earlier in the discussion of challenges faced by multiracial children and adolescents continues and permeates societal forces that multiracial individuals face at all developmental levels. Giving multiracial people the opportunity to check only one race or "Other" to indicate their racial heritage on registration forms is a form of institutionalized racism.

This section addresses the challenges faced by multiracial individuals in maintaining a balanced psychological adjustment and tells of triumphs in meeting these challenges. Multiracial adults who come for counseling often tell of painful memories of being teased or ostracized when they were younger. They may recall an ongoing feeling of "differentness" and loneliness or express feelings of guilt over rejection of part of their racial heritages. Some may have engaged in "passing" to escape the detrimental impact of race (Williams, 1997). Several of the multiracial participants in our research reported getting stared at even as adults, being looked at suspiciously by police, being treated as Black because of dark skin color, and hearing jokes about their appearance. Others indicated they have never heard racist remarks about their appearance.

Societal forces have a powerful influence on deciding the racial reference group identity of the multiracial individual. Williams (1996) notes that "By the time one has become an adult, one's racial membership within a hierarchically structured racialized society has been concretized" (p. 199). Added to this are the uncertainties of being accepted by people of one's biracial or multiracial heritages, thus making it even more challenging for the multiracial adult to resolve the identification issue (Houston, 1997; Spickard, 1997).

Some people in the larger society believe that mixed-race people are free to choose their racial self-identification. The reality is, however, that both men and women of mixed-race heritage will have their racial identification assigned based largely on their physical appearance (Root, 1990, 1997b).

Herring (1999) describes his biracial identity search and the cognitive dissonance and discrimination he experienced in attempting to integrate his mother's American Indian Cherew tribal affiliation with his father's White ancestry. Because of his White appearance, Herring was assumed to be White. After amassing enough evidence to be enrolled as a member of the Cherew tribe and being recruited for affirmative action programs, Herring's White appearance sometimes led to not being selected for these programs because he did not "look like an Indian." Being challenged to prove his biracial identity has been a common experience for Herring. Adams (1997) defines this as "racial legitimacy testing" (p. 62).

Context and social class also came into play with Herring's identity search, which began in southeastern North Carolina during the beginnings of the Civil Rights movement. As a "linthead" (a child of textile factory workers), he had to "buck the system" to enroll in college preparatory classes and to be selected for a major role in the junior class play.

Root (1990) states that "mixed race men will have a more difficult time overcoming social barriers than mixed race women" (p. 196). She believes that mixed-race men have to work harder to prove themselves to the majority White population while experiencing oppression from minority group men. Because women in general are seen as less threatening than men, mixed-race women may face less direct oppression.

The pressures to identify with only one of their racial heritages may not stop just because the individuals are no longer adolescents (Bowles, 1993; Comas-Diaz, 1994; Hall, 1992; Root, 1992, 1994). Adults with some African American heritage who choose to claim all of their heritages may be seen by other Americans of African ancestry as traitors willing to destroy affirmative action programs (Page, 1996). Root (1997b) underscores Page's thoughts when she notes that some African American communities "will be suspicious of the person who also insists on identifying simultaneously as Asian American, interpreting the insistence on a way of disavowing or diminishing one's African American heritage" (p. 34). As noted in Chapter 1, Tiger Woods, the well-known golf pro, has faced similar experiences in attempting to claim all of his racial heritages.

Societal restrictions on giving the biracial LatiNegra freedom to choose her racial identity are delineated by Comas-Diaz (1994, 1996). As the daughter of Western Hemisphere African American and Latino parents, the LatiNegra is seen as Black by both paternal and maternal communities. "The LatiNegra constitutes a classic example of racial exclusion, marginality, and disconnection . . . many LatiNegras are caught in a cycle of oppression, discrimination, trauma and victimization, and are often subject to revictimization" (Comas-Diaz, 1994, pp. 36 and 57). The LatiNegra experiences stereotyping along both racial and gender lines; confusion and conflicts related to racial identity and connectedness; and feelings of shame, guilt, ambivalence, and low self-worth.

An issue rarely addressed in the literature on multiracial individuals is the influence of having a parent who is an immigrant to the United States. Carmen Salazar Lowhar (personal communication, April 8, 1998) called attention to the loss she has experienced through not learning Spanish, her father's first language. Moving from Panama to California at age 10, her father spoke no English. As an adult, because of his own language difficulties in childhood and the stigma attached to accented speech, her father was determined that his children would enter school speaking unaccented English. For this reason, he and his wife, whose English ancestors came to North America prior to the Revolutionary War, agreed to speak only English to their children. For Salazar Lowhar, not knowing Spanish has meant a very personal loss. Her father still thinks and conceptualizes his emotions in Spanish; consequently there is an aspect of him she will never fully know and understand. In addition, not knowing Spanish has cut her off from communication with members of her father's family who remained in Panama.

Some respondents to our research saw benefits to having parents who were immigrants. One felt that his parents placed more emphasis on school and hard work than nonimmigrant parents; this emphasis on success in academics encouraged the individual to excel. Another respondent saw the benefits of citizenship and of higher education as a result of having parents who were immigrants.

It would be incomplete to omit reports of other strengths that multi-racial individuals possess. Poussaint (1984) was one of the first to present a positive picture of multiracial young adults in his report of Boston area interviews with 37 interracial individuals between 17 and 35 years old. These interviewees believed that having more than one racial heritage made them "more objective toward life and less prone to strong biased feelings toward groups of people . . . more tolerant, objective and nonjudg-mental people [and helped them to] easily move in both worlds and have all kinds of friends" (p. 10).

Participants in our research of multiracial individuals affirm the re-sponses of Poussaint's early 1980s interviewees. Our respondents noted many advantages to being multiracial, such as having an increased sense of uniqueness; having more variety in their lives; enjoying the best of both worlds; experiencing opportunities to relate to people in the cultures of both of their parents; being able to move freely between the two groups as well as other groups; and being more open, accepting, tolerant, and sensitive to others. One individual put it this way:

> I had to find commonality with people, with experiences, and this has been a significant, I think, advantage for me because life for me is about finding commonality, building partnerships, finding connections with people, feeling a sense of belonging, [and] a sense of connectedness. (Benjamin John, per-sonal communication, May 11, 1998)

Racial and Ethnic Reference Group Identity Models for Multiracial Individuals

Racial reference group identity models that were developed in the 1960s and 1970s describe the stages and/or processes that individuals experience in acquiring a positive identification with their racial heritage. Negative emotions may be experienced as people go through the stages or phases of developing this identification. Early models of racial identity development were linear and delineated the path to establishing iden-tification with a single racial heritage. Limitations of applying the early racial identity development models to multiracial people have been noted by many researchers and theorists (e.g., Jacobs, 1977, 1992; Johnson, 1992; Kerwin & Ponterotto, 1995; Miller, 1992; Poston, 1990; Root, 1990, 1992, 1994, 1995, 1996, 1997a, 1997b, 1998). A discussion of some of the more recent models for biracial and multiracial identity development is included here.

Poston's Contributions to a Biracial Identity Model

Poston (1990) critiqued early models of racial identity development and listed their limitations:

1. No provisions are included for persons who have more than one racial heritage with which to identify.
2. Inclusion of stages in which individuals reject any (or all) of their racial heritages is not a healthy resolution of racial identity development for people with more than one racial heritage.
3. Assumptions that persons will be accepted into their minority culture (or cultures) of origin may be invalid for multiracial individuals who are not accepted into any of their parent cultures.

Based on his critique of racial identity development models, Poston (1990) presented a biracial identity development model describing the stages that the biracial person experiences in attaining an integrated, racial reference group identity:

1. *Personal Identity.* The individual is still a child and the sense of self is largely independent of his or her ethnic heritage.
2. *Choice of Group Categorization.* Biracial youth feel pressures to choose one racial orientation, but limited cognitive development makes it unlikely that a biracial identity will be chosen.
3. *Enmeshment/Denial.* A mixture of confusion, self-hatred, and guilt from pressures to choose one identity and to deny the other heritage is experienced. Negative feelings must be resolved to move to an appreciation of both racial backgrounds.
4. *Appreciation.* Individuals may still be identifying with the group chosen in the second stage, but they are working to learn more about and to value the racial roots of both parents.
5. *Integration.* "Individuals at this stage experience wholeness and integration" (Poston, 1990, p. 154).

Root's Contributions to Models for Inclusion of Multiple Identities

Root's (1990) "schematic metamodel" includes four equally healthy alternatives among which biracial persons can operate in resolving two racial identities. It is a spiral model that assumes that, in each of the four resolutions, individuals recognize both sides of their racial heritage and freely choose how they want to identify themselves. This model "takes into account the forces of socio-cultural, political, and familial influences on shaping the individual's experience of their biracial identity" (p. 186).

The four possible resolutions of biracial identity of Maria Root's (1990) model are:

1. *Accept the identity assigned by society.* This can be a positive choice if the individual is happy with this identity and has family support. When the individual moves to another part of the country, a different identity might be assigned, making this the most tenuous of the four possible resolutions.

2. *Identify with both racial groups.* This resolution is positive if it does not require a basic personality change for the individual to operate in different racial groups.

3. *Identify with a single racial group.* This resolution differs from the first alternative in that the biracial person chooses the racial group with which to identify. The choice can be positive if the person does not feel marginalized by the group with which she or he has identified and if the individual does not deny the other half of her or his racial heritage.

4. *Identify with a new racial group, a mixed race group.* This is a positive resolution if this new identification includes all parts of the person's racial heritage. The person may move freely among groups but identify him- or herself as of mixed racial heritage.

Other theorists and researchers besides Root have advocated for situational racial and ethnic reference group identification. Among those advocating for the freedom of multiracial people to choose their identity depending on the context are Alipuria (1990), Anderson (1993), Brown (1995), and Stephan and Stephan (1989, 1991).

In 1997, Root stated that the context in which multiracial identity is developed challenges existing racial identity development models in these ways:

1. It cannot be assumed that the multiracial individual can find refuge in any of his or her racial groups of origin because of the racism that may exist within these communities (similar to Poston's third limitation).

2. No consideration is given to the simultaneous impact on identity from other core factors such as gender, sexual orientation, socioeconomic class, or nationality. One's racial identity may be only one part of one's identity at a particular time and will not always be the individual's primary identity.

3. Early models have not addressed how core identities may change depending on context. Identities are fluid, with different identities coming to the foreground depending on the situational context.

4. Individuals sampled for the models have been limited by the historical context and the setting in which they were assessed.
5. No attention has been given to physical appearance and the role of phenotype on racial identification in the early racial identity models.
6. Multiracial individuals with some White heritage do not understand what it is to "live White" because their non-Whiteness surfaces and is questioned by others (Root, 1997b).

Root (1997b) recognized the need to move toward more complex models of identity development and proposed "an ecological model that focuses on the intersection of perceived significant experiences through the lenses of gender, class, regional history of race relations and generation" (pp. 36-37). Three nonlinear processes that may occur concurrently are integral to Root's perspectives on how multiracial people explore and integrate their identities:

1. *Exposure/absorption.* This process involves exploring new material and giving meaning to it through receiving input from others. Processes of either constructive or destructive differentiation are used in interpreting new material. In constructive differentiation, difference is used to add breadth and complexity to understanding the new material. In destructive differentiation, foreclosure occurs and precludes gaining a full understanding of the meaning of difference.
2. *Competition/stratification.* Categorization and reformulation of material occur during these processes. In individualistic societies, persons attempt to see themselves in the most favorable way. Competition and judgment are viewed in terms of what is inferior or superior in self-definitions rather than in terms of group or collective goals. This can lead to a focus on only one perspective as correct. "In its most extreme form, one can use this process to destroy those who do not affirm one's existence or challenge one's privileged position" (Root, 1997b, p. 36).
3. *Reflective appraisal.* Reflective appraisal uses hindsight to consider and give priority to what is important for the good of the whole rather than prioritizing individual goals. This occurs as individuals acknowledge their mortality or when they attempt to respond from a code of ethics.

Root continues to propose that the identity that will be preeminent at a given time for the mixed-race person will be determined by the situational context. "That identity can be situationally determined is not evidence of instability but might be evidence of situation saliency for certain roles, behaviors, and expressions of attitudes and beliefs" (Root, 1998, p. 277).

Root (1998) details a wide variety of variables that can affect the identity of multiracial Asians. Of importance are the historical conditions in the Asian country of origin at the time the Asian ancestor emigrated to the United States, historical conditions in the United States at the time the ancestor arrived as an immigrant, and historical conditions in the United States in the interim since arrival. Some other variables that can affect the identity of multiracial Asians are age, generation in the United States, gender and ethnicity of each parent, acceptance or rejection by both paternal and maternal family members, physical appearance, gender, and having or having reclaimed an Asian name.

Root (1998) offers a new and greatly expanded Ecological Identity Model (see Figure 3.1). This model is designed to represent the array of possible influences on the identity of multiracial Asian Americans at any given time. It is based on Root's years of investigation of multiracial Asian identity and on the research of others who have studied mixed-race Asian Americans (e.g., Hall, 1980, 1982; Johnson, 1992; Kich, 1992; Miller, 1992; Murphy-Shigematsu, 1987; Thornton, 1983).

It appears that Root's Ecological Identity Model (see Figure 3.1) is applicable also to other multiracial individuals in the United States besides mixed-race Asian Americans. It will be interesting to note how mixed-race identity theorists and researchers will respond to the applicability of Root's Ecological Model for other mixed-race U.S. individuals.

Jacobs's Model of Biracial Identity Development in Black-White Children

Jacobs (1977, 1992) proposed that the Black-White child experiences three stages in the development of a biracial identity. Jacobs's model is based on the use of a doll-play instrument that he developed for use in interviews with biracial Black-White children. He recognizes that multiracial identity development for children who are not Black-White may differ from this three-stage model. Presentations of Jacobs's model at professional meetings in both the United States and Canada by the senior author have led to affirmation of Jacobs' model by multiracial individuals of other mixed-race backgrounds.

1. *Stage I, Pre-Color Constancy: Play and Experimentation with Color.* Biracial Black-White children under the age of 4½ years experiment with dolls of different colors to develop families without evaluating the color of the dolls. These children can select a doll that is the same color as their

Gender

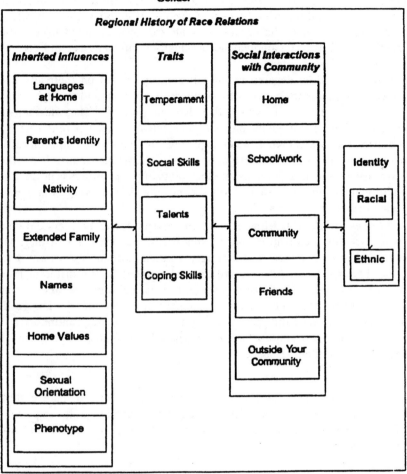

Figure 3.1. Ecological Identity
SOURCE: Root (1998), p. 279. Reprinted with permission.

skin, but they are not able to pick out dolls whose colors match the color of other family members.

   2. *Post-Color Constancy: Biracial Label and Racial Awareness.* At about 4½ years old, biracial Black-White children realize that their skin color will remain the same and begin to show an ambivalence about their own color. This ambivalence will be sequential, with children first showing

preference for Blackness and rejecting Whiteness, followed by preference for Whiteness and rejecting Blackness. Jacobs (1992) sees this ambivalence as necessary so that "discordant elements can be reconciled in a unified identity" (p. 210). The ambivalence gradually diminishes as children move through the second stage.

Biracial children develop racial self-concepts based on their advanced understanding that their own color will remain constant and through acquiring a biracial label with which they feel comfortable. They develop the concept of color constancy on their own but may need parental help in acquiring the biracial label. After acquiring a biracial label, children recognize that their parents are from two different racial groups. Perceptual distortion in selecting dolls that are the colors of their siblings is normal. An additional characteristic of Jacobs's second stage is a growing awareness of racial discrimination in society.

3. *Biracial Identity.* Biracial children between 8 and 12 years old come to at least three realizations during this period: (a) the color of their skin is related to their mixed-race heritage, (b) their skin color does not determine their race, and (c) they are biracial because of the different racial heritages of their parents. In this stage, biracial children are able to make accurate skin color choices for all members of their family. The earlier ambivalence toward the racial heritages of their parents continues to diminish, although it may surface again when the individual experiences the identity crises of adolescence.

Jacobs emphasizes the importance of parental efforts to help children know both sides of their racial identity. He also acknowledges the importance of other environmental and institutional influences on biracial identity development.

Phinney's Three-Stage Model of Adolescent Ethnic Identity Development

After years of researching many aspects of ethnic identity development with diverse populations of young people (Phinney, 1989; Phinney, 1990; Phinney, 1992; Phinney & Alipuria, 1990; Phinney & Chavira, 1992; Phinney & Tarver, 1988), Phinney (1993) presented her three-stage model of ethnic identity development in adolescence. This model is applicable to adolescents with either monoracial or multiracial identities.

Stage 1. *Unexamined ethnic identity.* Young people in this stage have not explored their ethnic identity. Two possible substages are (a) diffuse: No interest has been shown in ethnic identity and (b) foreclosed: Adolescents have let the opinions of others dominate their views on ethnic identity choice.

Stage 2. *Ethnic identity search/moratorium.* Adolescents in this stage are actively searching for information on their ethnic heritages and trying to understand what ethnicity means to them. They are not yet ready to choose an ethnic identity for themselves.

Stage 3. *Achieved ethnic identity.* Individuals at this stage are clear and confident about all aspects of the ethnic identity (or identities) they have chosen.

Kerwin-Ponterotto Biracial Identity Development Model

This model is based on Kerwin's 1991 qualitative dissertation research (Kerwin, Ponterotto, Jackson, & Harris, 1993) and on the integration of information from models by Jacobs (1977, 1992); Kich (1992); LaFromboise, Coleman, and Gerton (1993); Stephan (1992); and Williams (1992). It "presents an integrated framework for viewing the complex process that many individuals go through in developing their own racial identity" (Kerwin & Ponterotto, 1995, p. 210). Each person's resolution of this identity process is unique and is a lifelong process. Exposure to people of diverse racial heritages influences the process.

The Kerwin-Ponterotto model consists of six stages:

1. *Preschool.* During the preschool years up to 5 years of age, biracial children become increasingly aware of similarities and differences in the appearances of other people.
2. *Entry to school.* When children begin to be asked what they are, they usually define themselves in physically descriptive terms, such as the color of their skin. If parents have helped these children acquire a self-identification biracial label, the children may say they are "mixed" or use another term indicating they are aware of their full racial heritage.
3. *Preadolescence.* Young people become increasingly aware of physical appearance, skin color, and culture as determinants of racial group membership. They know that their parents belong to different racial groups. Self-identification is usually in terms of race, ethnicity, and/or religious background. A triggering event, such as entry into a racially integrated school or the experience of racist behavior, seems to precipitate full awareness of their biracial status.

4. *Adolescence.* Because racial identity becomes such an important part of overall identity development, this may be the most challenging time for biracial
   adolescents. Extreme pressure to identify with only one of their racial heritages
   may be felt, but these pressures may be neutralized by participation in sports
   or special academic interest groups.
5. *College/young adulthood.* Affiliation may be mainly with individuals of one
   of the person's racial heritages. As biracial individuals mature, there is an
   increasing tendency to reject the pressure to "choose one." There is a growing
   awareness of being biracial and bicultural and having the ability to perceive
   situations from more than one perspective.
6. *Adulthood.* Biracial adults continue to explore their biracial heritages and to
   integrate different aspects of their racial identity. Through the process of
   integration, biracial individuals find that they can function effectively in a
   variety of situations.

Carter's Views on Biracial
Identity Development

Carter (1995) proposes that an individual can develop a biracial identity
provided that the person integrates and values both parts of her or his racial
self. This biracial identity must be developed on a psychological base in
which neither racial heritage is compromised. To build this psychological
foundation, "a person who is biracial should become grounded in the deval-
ued racial group as a foundation for facilitating the merger of the two racial
groups" (Carter, 1995, p. 120).

Other Research Related to
Multiracial Identity

Adams (1997) researched developmental correlates and themes of racial
and ethnic identity development among 73 multiracial adults. Most of the
participants had experienced some form of racial or ethnic legitimacy testing from people in their racial heritages, but self-esteem was *not* related
to racial or ethnic legitimacy testing. Statistical support was obtained between ethnic identity and self-esteem and between family support of multiraciality and self-esteem. Two concepts that emerged as statistically significant predictors of multiethnic and multiracial identity were racial diversity
of home neighborhood in which the person was raised and family support of
multiraciality.

Saenz, Hwang, Aguirre, and Anderson (1995) noted that children of
Asian-Anglo background make up the largest segment of multiracial children
in the United States. Saenz et al. (1995) researched the extent to which Asian

identification persists among children of mixed-race families in which one parent is from the majority culture (Anglo) and one from the minority culture (Asian). Using data from the 1980 California Public Use Microdata Sample, parental choices of children's ethnic identity were categorized according to Anglo conformity, cultural pluralism (identifying as Asian), or melting pot (identifying as Amerasian, Other, or Other Asian). Overall, the results showed that children's exposure to culture, attributes of the parent, and geographic area of residence influence the construction of ethnic identity of these children. The majority of mixed-race children with an Asian Indian, Korean, Filipino, or Japanese parent were identified as having an Anglo identity. Children of Chinese-Anglo heritages were the least likely to be identified as Anglo-American. It appears that Chinese-Anglo children are strongly influenced by Chinese relatives to retain their Chinese identity.

Implications for Counseling Multiracial Individuals and Families

The delineation of issues of multiracial individuals of all ages, as well as the wealth of research just reviewed, alludes to many implications for counselor work with individuals and families with more than one racial heritage. The following list summarizes and highlights some implications for counselor interventions with these people. Implications are not listed in hierarchical order and are not mutually exclusive.

1. Listen for the strengths that multiracial individuals and families bring to counseling. Give feedback to individuals and families on these strengths. Help the individuals and families see how they can use these strengths in everyday living and problem solving.
2. Avoid viewing multiracial clients from a stereotypical perspective. Strive to understand and work with each person of mixed race as a unique individual.
3. Help parents to understand the development of multiracial identity in children and adolescents and encourage parents to engage their families in multiracial identity growth-producing activities. Family support and assistance is needed for mixed-race children and adolescents to develop positive multiracial identities. Parental assistance seems especially important in helping multiracial children choose a name for their multiracial identity (Jacobs, 1977, 1992).

Root's listing of actions (1997a) that parents of mixed-race children can take to help their children take pride in their Filipino heritage can be paraphrased as follows to include advice to parents of all mixed-race children:

    a. Give mixed-race children a first and/or middle name that is connected to their heritages.

    b. Be positive when you talk to children about their heritages.

    c. Help your mixed-race children learn about their different racial heritages through telling them stories of relatives from these heritages. Develop a family tree and encourage reading literature from these heritages. "Being connected to the past is a foundation for who you are in the present" (Root, 1997a, p. 91).

    d. Participate in cultural and community gatherings of the family's racial heritages. The children may find other mixed-race children at these events.

    e. Do not make remarks that denigrate any people of color.

    f. Determine if the children have been asked questions like "Who are you?" or "What are you?" Counselors should help parents learn how to work with their children to develop answers that will give the mixed-race children control over their environment.

4. Discuss the diversity of settings in which multiracial families and individuals operate. Exposure to people of different racial groups through residential neighborhoods and/or diversity of school or work settings helps multiracial people feel more comfortable with their identities.

5. Recognize that there are many components to a multiracial individual's core identity and that there is a fluidity among these components. Racial identity will not be the most important identity component at all times (Root, 1997b, 1998). Changing contexts will bring different components of identity to the forefront at different times for multiracial clients. Counselors can play an important role in helping multiracial clients explore all of their core identities.

6. Be aware of the variety of multiracial identity models in existence, but also be aware that there is no one correct model for use in all situations. Ecological models that recognize the impact of the total environment seem to be particularly helpful. Choice of concepts from models for work on multiracial identity resolutions will be specific to the situation and context of issues brought by multiracial individuals and families to counseling.

7. Use culturally sensitive active listening with multiracial clients of any age because multiracial individuals often feel that no one really understands what they are experiencing (Wehrly, 1996). Some multiracial adults have never shared their intense feelings of aloneness, differentness, guilt, rejection, anger, disappointment, and/or despair with anyone before coming for counseling.

8. Assist multiracial clients in locating a support group. If there is no multiracial support group in the immediate area, counselors can initiate steps to form such a group.

9. Be aware that negative perceptions of their physical appearance may be an important, but unspoken, issue for multiracial clients. Once rapport is established, this can be a critical issue for counselor-client exploration.

10. Listen for themes of confusion and victimization. Both confusion and victimization can stand in the way of resolving issues.

Summary

This chapter opened with a discussion of issues of multiracial individuals across the lifespan, from childhood through adulthood. Reports of research on racial identity development for multiracial people and multiracial identity models followed. The chapter closed with a listing of the counseling implications that follow from issues brought by the multiracial population and recent research on multiracial identity and mental health.

4

Other Multiracial Families

This chapter is devoted to an examination of the significant issues of families that have become multiracial through foster home placement and through cross-racial or transracial adoption. Issues of cross-racial adoption both from inside the United States and from foreign countries are included. Manuscripts addressing the United States' transracial adoption debate, which has been ongoing for more than a quarter of a century, are reviewed. Also addressed are pertinent issues of gay and lesbian multiracial families. The terms *multiracial, cross-racial,* and *transracial* are used synonymously. *Inracial placement* refers to the assignment of children to homes in which the adults are of the same race as the children.

There is an enormous dearth of counseling literature on the topics addressed in this chapter. We, the authors, are writing from our own work, from clinical observations of and discussions with peers and graduate students, and from extrapolation of concepts and issues raised by other professionals in the helping services.

Issues of Families That Have Become Multiracial Through Foster Home Placement

Children who are placed in foster home care are usually given very little notice of the major changes that are to take place in their lives. The children may experience shock, fright, loneliness, loss, denial, anger, and grief because of the abrupt changes that take place in their lives. This host of negative feelings may be exacerbated when they are placed in a home where the parenting figures are of a different racial heritage than their own. In many cases, an additional risk factor affecting transracial foster care placement is the lack of preparation of foster home families and foster children for transracial placement.

The placement of children with multiracial heritage in foster homes where neither parent is multiracial also adds to the potential for stress in the placement. Multiracial adolescents who have been in foster home care for years may experience intense feelings of insecurity and abandonment from being moved from foster home to foster home. "Their interracial status can put them in the 'double jeopardy' of not knowing where they fit racially nor where they fit in the societal structure (because they have never known a permanent home that they can call their own)" (Wehrly, 1996, p. 100).

Families who accept foster children into their homes represent a wide spectrum of family types. Some families have children of their own and accept only one foster child. Many families accept more than one foster child. Some families specialize in keeping babies until they are eligible for adoption. Others accept children within certain age ranges. Single parents head some foster homes; other foster homes are headed by more than one adult. Families of all ethnic and racial backgrounds provide foster home care.

The original foster home concept was to provide temporary homes for children whose parents were facing a crisis situation. Family service professionals were to work with parents to implement reunification of children with their birth parents at the earliest possible time. In contemporary foster homes, there may be a considerable amount of "coming and going" of foster children, so feelings of living in a secure and predictable environment may be absent.

Each foster home, whether transracial or nontransracial, is unique. It is important to be aware of stereotypes of cultures when considering factors related to transracial placements. Culture can have a powerful influence on the atmosphere of the home and on the way children are socialized into that culture (Wehrly, 1995). The traditional values of some cultures place much more emphasis on religion, rituals, and/or spirituality than other cultures. Both verbal and nonverbal communication are affected by culture. The volume and amount of communication in the home can also be influenced by culture. Transracial placement can lead to culture shock on the part of both the child and the foster parents, but it is important to study each situation before coming to conclusions about conflicts related to culture in transracial placements.

The professional helping service literature on work with children and families in transracial foster home placements is almost nonexistent. A 1993 report by Folaron and Hess is one professional report on transracial foster home placement. It details findings from a longitudinal study of foster home placement of children with mixed African American and Caucasian heritage and sheds light on changes needed by the child welfare system in transracial foster placement.

To work as a team with child welfare workers, counseling professionals can profit from self-examination related to the issues raised through the recommendations that follow from this research. Some of the implications for change include expectations of counselor roles in social advocacy. Implementing these roles may require that counselors participate in additional professional development.

Folaron and Hess (1993) found that child welfare workers were not adequately prepared to work with mixed-race families. Nor were they prepared to carry out investigations of racism in potential foster homes or to give attention to the racial composition of the foster caregivers' neighborhood, school, or religious organizations.

Professional preparation was recommended for child care workers, starting with the development of self-awareness and the clarification of personal values. Additional professional preparation of child care practitioners for transracial foster home placement work was outlined. Skills in detecting prejudice and racism in the foster home family milieu were emphasized because "Subtle prejudices and blatant racism in foster families will seriously undermine a child's self concept" (Folaron & Hess, 1993, p. 122).

Recommendations for assessment of potential foster families for placement of mixed-race children included several dimensions: the motivations of the family for choosing to accept mixed-race children, the racial background of members of the foster family (including other foster children in the home), attitudes and opinions of the foster family about mixed-race people, frequency of contact with people of other races and the nature of these contacts, feelings regarding visits from family members of the mixed-race foster child, availability of appropriate multicultural literature in the home, racial composition of the neighborhood, racial composition of the school that the mixed-race children will attend, and support within the school for helping the child to develop a positive multiracial identity (Folaron & Hess, 1993). It was emphasized that a color-blind approach to this assessment perpetuates racism. Each of these assessment recommendations seems applicable to preparation needed for all cross-racial foster care placement.

Accurate figures on the number of children in foster care are difficult to obtain, but it is known that many of the thousands of children in foster and other out-of-home care have been waiting for placement in same-race homes (Goetz, Barstow, Farrell, & Palya, 1998; Griffith & Silverman, 1995; Winik, 1998). Many of the children waiting in foster care are African American because their numbers exceed the number of approved African American adoptive homes.

Federal Legislation Regarding *Reasonable Efforts* to Reunify Families

Nearly two decades ago, federal legislation required states to make *reasonable efforts* to "reunify children placed in foster care with their families of origin by providing counseling, substance abuse treatment services, housing assistance and other appropriate services" (Goetz et al., 1998). A major problem with this regulation was that what constituted *reasonable efforts* was never defined. Critics argued that some states placed too much emphasis on extended reunification efforts that were not in the best interests of children because the efforts put them "in limbo" in foster care for years.

The experiences of Diane, a White foster parent who took in premature Black twins and lost them to their birth mother when the mother returned and went through treatment, chronicles the chaos of the *reasonable efforts* system and its failure to put limits on the length of time that efforts were made to rehabilitate the mother (Finkel, 1997). The twins had been abandoned at birth, hospitalized for multiple medical problems for 14 months, and released to foster care with Diane, who raised them as her own children for 3½ years. At the time the hospital released the twins to Diane for foster care, Diane was led to believe she could eventually adopt them. Child psychiatrist Marilyn Binoit critiqued the experience: "Three and a half years? . . . and then the biological mother gets the children back? You have now disrupted the emotional development of those children. You, the court, have created a new abandonment" (Finkel, 1997, p. 11).

New guidelines for transracial adoption were distributed by the Department of Health and Human Services in April 1995. These guidelines followed from Congressional passage of the Multiethnic Placement Act late in 1994 (Goetz et al., 1998). The Multiethnic Placement Act emphasized the "best interest of the child" as the central factor in adoption. Race, color, or national origin of the child or adoptive parents could be considered in the total context of best interest of the child but could no longer be the primary factor in placing an adoptable child.

Modifications of the Multiethnic Placement Act of 1994 came about as a result of legislation in August 1996. Tax credits were allowed for qualified adoption expenses to families with incomes not exceeding $75,000 (Hollingsworth, 1998).

The Federal Adoption and Safe Families Act signed into law on November 19, 1997 limits the duration of the "in limbo" period for rehabilitation of parents and reunification with their children (Goetz et al., 1998). Federal support for counseling, substance abuse treatment, and other services to help reunify parents with their children is cut to 15 months after removal of the child from the home. In addition, states are mandated to begin proceedings to terminate parental rights and make children eligible for adoption when a child has been in foster care for 15 of the preceding 22 months. Court procedures involving the welfare of the child are open to input from foster and preadoptive parents, relative caregivers, and the child's biological parents. The 1997 law clarifies that the *reasonable efforts* mandate is not applicable in cases where the "child has been subjected to 'aggravated circumstances,' such as chronic abuse and neglect, sexual abuse, or when the parent has killed or assaulted another child in their care" (Goetz et al., 1998, p. 10).

The 1997 Federal Adoption and Safe Families Act is designed to expedite the process of making children of color lingering in foster homes available for adoption and to provide financial incentives to locate permanent homes. The legislation also states that race cannot be the primary factor in placing children for adoption (Goetz et al., 1998).

Issues of Families That Have Become Multiracial Through Transracial Adoption Within the United States

Transracial adoption within the United States has gone through turbulent times since the early 1970s (Waldman & Caplan, 1994). An ongoing national debate about the appropriateness of placing children of color in White homes has led to a drastic curtailment of transracial placements. Because this major professional disagreement remains unsettled, the next section will include a brief summary of the history of restrictions on transracial placements and review some of the dozens of professional publications that address the issues of transracial adoption in the United States.

Professional Responses to Restrictions on Transracial
Foster Home and Adoptive Placements

In most states, there have been attempts to place foster and adoptive children of color in homes where the racial heritage of the parents is the same as that of the child. In the early 1970s, the National Association of Black Social Workers (NABSW) went on record as unconditionally opposed to transracial foster home placement and transracial adoption of Black and mixed-race Black children, stating that this form of transracial adoption would lead to cultural genocide (McRoy & Hall, 1996). The position taken by the NABSW led to a large curtailment of transracial placements of Black and mixed-race Black children.

In 1978, the Indian Child Welfare Act set federal standards for removing Indian children from their homes and gave Indian tribes exclusive jurisdiction over adoptions of Indian children eligible for tribal membership (McRoy & Hall, 1996). Prior to 1978, transracial placements of Native American children had been high in many areas of the United States. After the Indian Child Welfare Act, there was a dramatic decline in transracial placement of Indian children.

Following the NABSW statement opposing transracial adoption of Black children and the 1978 Indian Child Welfare Act, there has been a plethora of publicity on the pros and cons of transracial adoption. Papers addressing transracial adoptions of African American or mixed-race children with some African American heritage dominated the press. Some of these position papers and research reports will be highlighted here.

A 1981 report of the study of transracial adjustment of Black children adopted by White families by Silverman and Feigelman indicated that initially the transracial adoptees seemed more maladjusted. When age of placement was considered, the adjustment differences disappeared. The authors recognized that "the most decisive element in influencing children's maladjustment scores is the child's age at adoption" (Silverman & Feigelman, 1981, p. 535).

Early 1980s studies of self-esteem and racial identity in transracial and inracial Black adoptees found no differences in self-esteem among the transracial and inracial adoptees (McRoy & Zurcher, 1983; McRoy, Zurcher, Lauderdale, & Anderson, 1982). However, transracially adopted children seemed to have more of a problem with their racial identity than the inracial adoptees.

Shireman and Johnson's 1986 report of an 8-year longitudinal study of adoptions of Black infants into three types of homes (single parent, transracial, and inracial) indicated that overall adjustments for Black infants placed in the three types of adoptive homes were almost identical. Another report on the same study (Johnson, Shireman, & Watson, 1987) presented two divergent interpretations of the data. Shireman recognized that there is no question that Black homes are preferable for Black children. However, she continued to support transracial adoption for Black children as long as they are having to grow up in foster rather than permanent homes. Watson pointed out that transracially adopted Black children became assimilated into the White families over the years. In the process of this assimilation, their development of a Black racial identity became less and less important. Watson felt that transracially adopted Black children's sense of their Black racial identity stops growing at about age 8 years; Black racial identity development continues to grow for Black children who are inracially adopted.

A 1993 report by Kallgren and Caudill evaluated transracial adoption practices in four major metropolitan areas to determine if the agencies were "placing transracial adoptees at an early age, educating adoptive parents about the need to create a racially aware family setting, counseling adoptive parents on racial identity issues, and evaluating the racial awareness of the prospective adoptive parents" (p. 553). Positive findings of the Kallgren and Caudill study were that agencies were implementing transracial adoptions at an early age, evaluating the ability of the adopters to accept and live with racial differences, and counseling about the transracial adoptees' formation of a racial identity and about community reactions to the transracial adoption.

Despite an awareness of the importance of a racially aware context in an adoptive home, agencies were sometimes falling short on meeting these needs of transracial adopters: (a) need for counsel about extended family reactions, (b) need to live in a racially mixed neighborhood and to have the children attend a racially integrated school, (c) need for training sessions for transracial adoption and adequate literature on the transracial adoption process, and (d) need to form support groups for transracial adopters to get together to share experiences. Similarities exist between the findings of the Kallgren and Caudill (1993) study of transracial adoption practices and the Folaron and Hess (1993) study of foster home placements of mixed-race children reviewed earlier in this chapter.

Accounts by J. Douglas Bates in his 1993 book *Gift Children: A Story of Race, Family, and Adoption in a Divided America* support the recommendations made by Kallgren and Caudill (1993). *Gift Children* is a 23-year family autobiography of the transracial adoption of two daughters (Lynn, a biracial African American-White child, and Liska, an African American child) into the White Euro-American Bates family that consisted of Bates, his wife, and two sons. In retrospect, Bates recognized how much pre- and postadoptive counseling might have helped the family to work with Lynn and Liska to encourage pride in their racial identity. Living mostly in all-White neighborhoods, the daughters felt racially isolated in their schools, had little help in developing Black pride, and had minimal help in learning to cope with racism. On the positive side, Lynn and Liska developed the ability to bridge the two cultures and did much to help their adopted brothers, parents, and extended family members to grow with them to a broader worldview that transcended race.

For more than 20 years, Simon and associates engaged in longitudinal research of transracially adopted children, their families, and the communities into which they were adopted (Simon & Alstein, 1992; Simon, Alstein, & Melli, 1994). The research began in 1972 when the adoptive children and their parents were involved in in-depth interviews. Follow-up interviews were conducted in 1979, 1984, and 1991. The 1994 report grouped the researchers' findings under these categories: (a) Parent Socioeconomic Characteristics; (b) Birth and Adoption Patterns; (c) Neighborhoods, Schools, and Friends; (d) The Adoption Experience; (e) The Parents' Reactions; and (f) The Children's Reactions.

Simon, Alstein, and Melli (1994) stated that the basic findings of their research did not support the NABSW warnings that transracially adopted children will grow up confused about their racial identity. The researchers recommended subsidizing adoption so that more minority foster parents could become adoptive parents. A strong plea was issued that the best interest of the child be the most important criterion in transracial adoptive procedures (Simon, Alstein, & Melli, 1994).

Collmeyer (1995) traced the history of the adoption efforts of the Boys and Girls Aid Society of the state of Oregon from 1944 to 1977. In the years covered in this report, a total of 466 children of color (Asian American, Native Americans, and African Americans) were placed, some inracially and some transracially. Collmeyer's report underscored the importance of a diverse adoption agency staff and the involvement of people of color in achieving success in both inracial and transracial adoption practices.

Griffith and Silverman (1995) published an extensive review of the professional literature (including legal cases) related to transracial adoptions. The authors pointed out that even though the transracial adoption of Black children by White families makes up only about 1% of all adoptions, the practice "generates substantial commentary and thought, possibly because it forces us to confront the basic question of how we link families and racial identity" (p. 98).

Griffith and Silverman (1995) also note that even though the Equal Protection Clause in the Fourteenth Amendment of the U.S. Constitution prohibits discrimination based on race, race was used to decide who was permitted to adopt in some court cases. The authors conclude: "As a society, we apparently believe that racial discrimination is acceptable in the context of establishing families, although we will generally not tolerate racial discrimination in other contexts" (p. 112). Also recognized was the fact that special interest groups on both sides of the transracial adoption debate continue to ignore the results of scholarly research in the field. A strict time limit on a search for adoptees' relatives was recommended, but this search is not to constitute a preference for same-race placement.

McRoy and Hall (1996) presented an overview of U.S. transracial adoptions from the mid-20th century through the early 1990s. Various perspectives on racial and ethnic identity development of transracial adoptees are included, along with implications for therapy for transracial adoptees.

In May 1996, the *Journal of Black Psychology* published a special section that included nine manuscripts on transracial adoption. Alexander and Curtis (1996) wrote the opening paper, "A Review of Empirical Research Involving the Transracial Adoption of African American Children." Responses to and discussion of the Alexander and Curtis position paper were authored by Abdullah, Goddard, Gopaul-McNicol, Harrison, Lovett-Tisdale and Purnell, Penn and Coverdale, Turner and J. Taylor, R. Taylor and Thornton, and Willis (all 1996).

All of the respondents felt that Alexander and Curtis' critical review of empirical investigations of transracial adoption of African American children was an important contribution to the transracial adoption literature. Some of the respondents disagreed with the conclusions of Alexander and Curtis that "No empirical evidence exists to demonstrate that such placements are harmful to the mental health of African American children" (Alexander & Curtis, 1996, pp. 232-233). More research stressing the importance of the adoptee's culture-group identity was recommended.

Many of the respondents to Alexander and Curtis's (1996) article felt that the research and adoption industry is controlled by White European values that influence interpretations of research. Several suggestions were made for other alternatives than transracial adoption: improving family assistance so the children can stay with their birth families; more use of Black extended families; and more innovative, aggressive adoption policies to increase the numbers of Black adoptive families.

McRoy, Oglesby, and Grape (1997) discussed issues related to inracial adoption of African American children and echoed many of the concepts presented by the respondents to the Alexander and Curtis (1996) article. McRoy et al. (1997) discussed how barriers to same-race placement for African American adoptees are related to factors such as the lack of minority and culturally trained adoption agency staff, availability of approved Caucasian adoptive families, costs involved in the adoption process, and changing state and federal adoption policies. Successful same-race adoption programs in California and Texas were described.

Romanc (1997) described a bold new adoption plan that uses adoption parties to introduce prospective adoptive parents to children trapped in foster home care. Most of the children are 6 years old or older; some are waiting for same-race placement. The program described by Romanc was sponsored by the Adoption Exchange of Denver and endorsed by the Child Welfare League of America, based in Washington, DC.

Hollingsworth (1997) reported on a meta-analytic review of six studies that examined "whether children of ethnic minority groups, reared in Caucasian families, can receive the racial and ethnic socialization and orientation that is necessary for them to be able to maintain adequate racial/ethnic identity and self esteem" (p. 108). Transracially adopted African American, Mexican American, and mixed-race children were included in the studies. All data had been obtained directly from the children. The analysis did not indicate a statistically significant effect on the self-esteem of transracial adoptees. In discussing the results of her meta-analysis, Hollingsworth (1997) predicted that future studies of transracial adoptions could be expected to show a moderate, negative effect on the racial and ethnic identity of the adoptees. Eleven suggestions for future research of transracial adoptees were presented.

After reviewing the history of transracial adoption, Hollingsworth (1998) concluded that the number of children of color listed as languishing in foster care is inaccurate, and lifting restrictions on transracial adoption is unnecessary. These six alternatives to transracial placement were proposed by Hollingsworth (1998):

1. Increase the number of foster families of color to increase the potential for same-race adoptions.
2. Revise adoptive agency policies to remove organizational barriers to recruitment and eligibility of families of color so that more of these families will come forward to adopt.
3. Get a more accurate count on the number of out-of-home placements of children who are eligible for adoption. Up to half of the children in out-of-

home placement have special needs that make them difficult to place and should not be counted among those lingering in foster care awaiting adoptive placement.

4. Eliminate the inequities that exist between services to White families and services to families of color in the child welfare system.

5. Do not include children of color in kinship foster care among the children who are available for adoption.

6. Increase services to families living below the poverty level to assist children in poverty to remain with their birth families.

The hundreds of pages of literature addressing the pros and cons of transracial adoption contain a minimum of information on the issues of the thousands of children caught up in this debate. Issues of in-country and out-of-country adoptive children, as well as issues of adoptive parents and counselor involvement in addressing these issues, are summarized in the last section of this chapter.

Intercountry Transracial Adoption

Intercountry or out-of-country adoption (adopting from another country) has followed each of the major wars in the 20th century (Register, 1991). Following World War I, a group of women in Britain and Scandinavia formed the Save the Children organization to find homes for Belgian orphans. Following World War II, the officially organized U.S. Committee for the Care of European Children brought 300 unaccompanied minor children from Europe. Most of the first group were Polish children, but in the years that followed World War II, orphan children were admitted to the United States from Germany, Greece, and Italy.

Following the Korean conflict, a new chapter in intercountry adoption occurred. Some of the adoptable Korean children had been made orphans during the war. However, many of the children made available for adoption from Korea since the early 1950s were Amerasian or Eurasian children who had been fathered by United Nations troops in Korea. The children's physical appearance reflected their biracial heritage and made it very difficult for their mothers to raise their biracial children in a country with a strong patrilineal value system in which the child's identity comes through the father and is recorded in a patriarchal lineage that extends back hundreds of years. A major exodus of Korean or part-Korean babies and children to the United States followed.

During and following the United States' involvement in Southeast Asia, a similar situation occurred, and large numbers of Southeast Asian and Amerasian babies and children emigrated to the United States. Many of those coming in the 1980s were older Amerasian children who came in search of their fathers. The adoptions of out-of-country babies and children following World War I, World War II, the Korean War, and the Southeast Asian conflict were prompted largely on humanitarian grounds. Families adopted because they had been encouraged to make room for children in need of homes.

Additional factors have given impetus to out-of-country adoptions in the United States since the mid-1970s. More widespread use and effectiveness of contraceptive devices, an increase in abortions, and the tendency of single mothers to keep their children resulted in fewer White babies available for adoption. In addition, the strong antitransracial adoption statement of the NABSW in 1972 and the 1978 Indian Child Welfare Act led to a large decline in the number of babies available for in-country transracial adoption. Because of the decline in adoptable babies and children in the United States, childless couples and, more recently, single adults have made arrangements to adopt children from outside the United States.

Intercountry adoptees have been coming from South and Central America as well as from Eastern Europe and some of the Asian countries. Children have been made available for adoption in these countries for a variety of reasons, including abject poverty in their families of origin. Register (1991) summarized the situation of out-of-country adoptees in the past half century: "Each of the nearly 200,000 children who have found new families in the United States since the end of World War II has come with a life history marked by misfortune" (p. 3). She also noted that because most of these children are visibly different in appearance from their adoptive parents, it is common for these parents to hear, "Are those kids yours?"

"Those kids" are human beings who have crossed national and cultural borders to live with new families in the United States. Culture shock greater than the culture shock experienced in cross-racial foster home placement occurs. Babies coming from cultures where they are held or carried all day and where they sleep with their mothers at night to White U.S. families may experience the shock of spending much time alone in cribs or playpens rather than being held or carried. Some of the challenges faced by older children are grief from separation and loss of birth or foster care families, grief from the loss of their native country and its customs, drastic differences in both verbal and nonverbal communication, strange food, and the process of bonding and adjusting to new ways of living with their adoptive parents.

Register (1991) noted additional issues and themes that must be faced by out-of-country transracial adoptees and their U.S. adoptive families: recognizing that international adoption begins in tragedy, discussing questions of how and why the children were given away by their birth family, building a new life as an interracial family, and dealing with intrusive questions as to who the children are and to whom they belong. Constructing the family tree comes as a special challenge. Acquiring information on the cultural heritage that the adoptive children have left behind before the children reach adolescence is important so that the adoptive children will be better prepared for the identity crises that adolescents experience. In addition, the family that has become transracial through adoption needs to learn how to deal with stereotypes and racism and how White privilege operates. Learning the survival skills of U.S. minority families can be a daunting task.

Trolley, Wallin, and Hansen (1995) underscore the importance of adoptive families' acknowledging the adoptive status and birth culture of internationally adopted children. They outline educational, therapeutic, and research roles for mental health professionals working with these adoptive families.

Bartholet (1993) described her experiences in adopting internationally and how she came to recognize that racial thinking has dominated both in- and out-of-country adoptions. As a single, White, female lawyer, Bartholet reviewed the recent history of transracial adoption in the United States and described the lengthy, tedious, and sometimes uncertain bureaucratic process she experienced in adopting two children from Peru. Bartholet emphasized the critical importance of knowing the laws governing international adoption both in the United States and in the country from which the child is being adopted.

Wilkinson (1995), a Korean-born psychologist who has helped U.S. families adopting Korean children, addressed the importance of both psychological and legal processes in international adoption. Included were a detailed discussion of the psychological processes involved in out-of-country adoption and an overview of the legal process. Because this chapter has already noted psychological issues related to international adoption, a brief overview of the legal process will be included, with the caution that readers interested in the legal process must do a considerable amount of additional investigation to conform with U.S. local, state, and national regulations and the laws and regulations of the country from which the individual plans to adopt.

Highlights from Wilkinson's discussion are:

1. Adoption is governed by laws in the state in which the prospective adopter resides. A home study will be made over a period of time to explore several

aspects of the suitability of the home to receive an adoptive child. Reports of this home study are used both by officials in the United States and in the country in which the adoptee resides.

2. Federal laws govern Immigration and Naturalization Service (INS) requirements for sponsoring the immigration of an orphaned adoptive child to the United States. INS governs approval of the petition to adopt and the definition of an orphan.

3. Each country controls the process of international adoption. Some countries require that the adoption process be completed in their court systems before adoptive children are allowed to leave the home country. Methods of completing the adoption process vary by the regulations of each country.

4. Some states require a period of supervision and home visits after the international adoptee reaches the United States before finalizing the adoption process.

Wilkinson (1995) concludes: "Therapists working with couples who adopt internationally can assist them better by being aware of the legal procedures, pitfalls, and the psychosocial aspects and consequences" (p. 182).

Most families adopting from Latin America and Asia become multiracial and may have their first direct experience with racism following intercountry adoption. Some of the families portrayed in the book *Of Many Colors* (Kaeser & Gillespie, 1997) became multiracial through intercountry adoption. One interracial couple, the Harper/Johnsons, adopted children whose heritages are Korean, Guatemalan, Russian, and Caucasian. Marilyn Johnson, the mother, talks about race and how race really has very little to do with everyday life. She recognizes, however, that it is impossible to be colorblind: "If you say you don't see the color of your kids, then you're not really seeing them or accepting them for who they are" (Kaeser & Gillespie, 1997, p. 41).

The effects of international transracial adoption on both adoptees and adopters have been studied. Bagley's review of research on transracial adoption in several Western nations resulted in a recommendation that parents obtain as much information as possible on the social and biological history of prospective adoptees before adoption. Overall, the adjustment of transracially adopted children was good. Also emphasized by the authors reviewed by Bagley were the importance of preparing both the adoptive parents and the adoptive children for the transracial adoption and preparing the family to deal with racism. Two themes that emerged in the studies of the development of positive self-esteem in transracially adopted children were the importance of the basic warmth and love given by the adoptive parents and the provision of a predictable and consistent environment.

For nearly four decades, Korea served as a primary source of intercountry adoptees. Korean adoptees and their adoptive families have been studied in depth. Lydens's (1988) doctoral thesis is a longitudinal research study that examined self, ethnic, and adoptive identity development among 101 Korean adoptees at adolescence and early adulthood. These children were placed in U.S. homes in the late 1950s and early 1960s. The sample consisted of one group of Korean-born children adopted at 1 year old or earlier and a group that was adopted at 6 years or older. Both samples were surveyed as adolescents in 1974 and again as young adults in 1984. A consistent theme that emerged was that the beneficial effects of intercountry transracial adoption are stronger than possible negative effects for adoptees and their families. Adoptees developed normally and adjusted positively; they displayed normal identities at adolescence and maintained these identities into adulthood. Lydens (1988) concluded that "as long as the best interests of the child are considered paramount, no reasons emerged from this study which would discourage the policy of crosscultural adoption" (p. 137).

Alstein et al. (1994) reported on nationwide follow-up interviews of intercountry Korean adoptees and their adoptive parents. Twenty-nine adult foreign-born adoptees whose average age was 22 years and 23 sets of parents participated in phone interviews with master of social work students. "The students' main observations stressed individualizing adoptees and their families, cautioning against falling into the all-too-easy trap of self-fulfilling labeled behavior. A second theme was the importance of each social worker's own sensitivity and attitudes toward this type of racial mixing, and emphasized professional and personal self-awareness" (Alstein et al., 1994, p. 268).

Kim's 1995 case review of four decades of transracial international adoption of Korean children by families in the United States, the former West Germany, the Netherlands, Sweden, Denmark, and Norway supports findings of Lydens's (1988) report. "The overall impression is that Korean adoptees have done very well consistently, study after study, when surveying the literature spanning four decades and on both sides of the Atlantic" (Kim, 1995, p. 149). Kim suggested that the long history of Korea's well-organized preadoption and adoption arrangements and the resulting satisfactory adjustment of Korean adoptees in host countries can serve as a model for other nations now replacing Korea as the chief source of transracial international adoptees.

On a different focus, Gup (1997) discussed the "heavy load" that Asian children carry from stereotypes that they are "whiz kids." Gup has a special interest in the possible negative effect of these stereotypes, as he has adopted two sons from Korea.

L. DiAnne Borders, a counselor educator and a former editor of the *Journal of Counseling and Development,* adopted a son from Peru. Borders has added to the literature on international transracial adoption by single professional women and to the literature on developmental issues of international transracially adopted children (1995b). Borders (1993a) addressed the multiple decisions and issues that must be faced by the single parent professional female once she decides to adopt a child and (1993b) defended giving single professional women the right to adopt children. Questions that international transracially adopted children ask about adoption at various developmental stages and ways to help young children learn about their birth culture are also discussed by Borders (1995a).

Issues of Gay and Lesbian Transracial Families

Included among the many multiracial families portrayed through both narrative and pictorial accounts in the book *Of Many Colors* (Kaeser & Gillespie, 1997) are stories of the lives of four lesbian or gay transracial families. A review of issues and concerns expressed by these four families follows.

The Benjamin/Zellers family includes an interracial lesbian couple and two sons. Eric is Black and the son of Sheila. Bonnie's biracial Black/White son was conceived through the use of a donor Black sperm. The family emphasizes the deep love they have for each other and the strength they have developed as an interracial diverse family. Concerns expressed by the family are the need to live in an area with more diversity, recognition of the fear that many in the mainstream have of both lesbian couples and young Black men, and the way many people distance themselves from their family because of this fear. In addition, the couple is concerned about how to raise their sons to channel their anger so that it does not destroy them.

The Elsa/Robinson family is a gay interracial couple who have two adopted Black sons. Michael notes that some people who see the Elsa/Robinson family are reminded of the issues that they have both with gay couples and with interracial relationships. "We strike up a lot of interest as a family because we touch other people's fears and prejudices just by our existence" (Kaeser & Gillespie, 1997, p. 29). Doug remembers how, in the 1950s and 1960s, his Black family was one of the first to integrate the town in which they lived and realizes that now, in the 1990s, he is helping gay families to be accepted. Doug believes people have changed and are coming to see that "it's not a big deal. . . . We're just like everybody else" (Kaeser & Gillespie, 1997, p. 30).

The Sbar interracial lesbian family includes Freda and her adopted Black daughter, Alannah. Freda described how she experienced her first racism soon after she adopted Alannah. While walking and carrying her new daughter in a baby carrier on her chest, two women she met called the baby a puppy. Freda immediately responded to let them know that the baby was not a puppy. At first, Freda's family had difficulties in accepting that she is a lesbian and that it was OK for her to adopt transracially. It took a visit to Freda's family with the adopted Alannah for the family to accept the baby as a member of the family. Freda recognizes that life for Alannah as the Black daughter of a White Jewish lesbian mother will not be easy. She believes that the special perspective she has gained on oppression and the strength and love she and her daughter have for each other will help to carry them through difficult times.

The Wheeler family consists of Dona, a lesbian mom, and two adopted children, a son from El Salvador and an African American daughter. Dona discusses the challenges of racism that her family faces and anticipates identity problems when the children reach adolescence as well as questions from her adopted son and daughter about why she adopted them.

There is a considerable body of professional counseling literature about counseling gay and lesbian people. Gay and lesbian families that have become multiracial through cross-racial partnering, in vitro fertilization, and/or transracial adopting have been ignored in the counseling literature. Some of the professional literature on gay and lesbian parenting sheds light on challenges these families face and alludes to issues that may be brought to counselors. Adding a cross-racial component to these families can make issues even more complex for gay and lesbian transracial families.

Myths about gay and lesbian parents still exist and continue to cloud the perspectives of not only the general public but some legal officials involved in custody cases. Gay and lesbian parents have experienced difficulties in obtaining custody of their children. Manuscripts that review the literature on adoption by gay and lesbian parents and child custody court cases when one of the parents is gay or lesbian (Cramer, 1986; Falk, 1989; McIntyre, 1994; Sullivan, 1995) reveal that these myths sometimes influence both the recommendations of professionals in the field of adoption and decisions made by magistrates. A brief discussion of some of these myths follows:

1. The molestation myth holds that gay and lesbian parents are more inclined to molestation of children as well as to involvement in inappropriate sexual

behavior in front of children. People who hold these beliefs are confusing pedophilia, a sexual disorder that is not related to sexual orientation, with gay or lesbian sexual preferences. Research on sexual exploitation by gay parents shows that this behavior is almost nonexistent and that "adult heterosexual males have a greater probability of sexually abusing children than do adult homosexual males" (McIntyre, 1994, p. 137).

2. A second myth proposes that children will develop homosexual preferences through living with gay parents and their lovers. Cramer (1986) states that "Although the development of sexual orientation is a complex and misunderstood process, the research seems to refute the notion that gay parents will produce gay children or disturbed children in numbers greater than might be expected of nongay parents" (p. 505).

3. A third myth is that all homosexual people are emotionally unstable and incapable of being good parents. The theory that homosexuality was related to mental illness was reviewed by the American Psychiatric Association Board of Trustees in the mid-1970s. Upon finding no evidence to support this theory, the Board unanimously voted to remove the term *homosexuality* from the list of mental disorders in the *Diagnostic and Statistic Manual (DSM)*.

4. The fourth fictitious belief relates to the myth just discussed. This myth holds that children raised by lesbians mothers are more likely to develop emotional or psychological problems. No direct relationship between the sexual orientation of the mother and the mental health of her offspring has been found (McIntyre, 1994).

5. Another belief about gay families is that children of a gay parent will suffer teasing and peer rejection. Investigations of this behavior do not show that it is a common occurrence. However, as the children grow into adolescence it becomes more common for the son or daughter to receive negative messages about their parents' sexuality. Cramer (1986) noted that children of gay parents did not feel free to talk with their peers about the uniqueness of their family. Neither did they feel support from peers if their gay parents broke up or separated.

Sullivan (1995) recognized that policy issues have become more open in relation to gay and lesbian adoption. She cautioned, however, that potential sources of prejudice against gay and lesbian adoption are still there and underscored the need for self-awareness and retraining of all staff involved in the adoption process. Transracial adoptive lesbian parents who participated in our research confirmed the subtle prejudice and racism that they have experienced.

Patterson (1992) published an extensive review of literature on issues of children of lesbian and gay parents. In 1997, Patterson published an updated treatise on the same topic. Her conclusion was that "There is no evidence to suggest that psychosocial development among children of gay men or lesbians is compromised in any respect relative to that among offspring of heterosexual parents" (p. 1036). The shortcomings of conducting research of this nature and implications for revision of well-known theories of psychosocial development were also addressed by Patterson (1997).

In some areas of the United States, and among some groups, gay and lesbian families face homophobia. When gay and lesbian families have the additional transracial component, homophobia may be heightened. A major challenge for the individuals in gay and lesbian transracial families is that of facing prejudice and racism.

Responding to Issues of Transracial
Adoptive Children and Parents

Some of the issues faced by both in-country and out-of-country transracial adoptive children and their parents are shared issues. For children as well as parents there are the challenges of cross-racial and cross-cultural adjustment. Counselors help with this adjustment through teaching parents and children about the impact of culture on everyday life (Wehrly, 1995).

Learning to face prejudice, racism, and oppression is a family challenge for the transracial adoptive family. For the multiracial gay or lesbian family, the prejudice and oppression may include the added challenge of homophobia. Counselors who work with adoptive families and their children help them decide when and how to deal with prejudice, racism, and oppression (Wehrly, 1996).

Helping a transracial adoptive family develop pride as a multiracial family encompasses both pre- and postadoptive counseling. School counselors can build a developmental multicultural program that celebrates diversity and assists in the acceptance of transracial adoptive children and their families (Wehrly, 1996). Agency counselors can also assist in building pride in the multiracial composition of the family.

Feelings of loss are felt by adoptive parents and their adoptive children but around different issues. Many adoptive parents go through grief and loss when they recognize they cannot have a "blood" child of their own. All adopted children at some time or other in their lives recognize that they were given away by their birth family. With this recognition may come a host of feelings, such as rejection, abandonment, loneliness, insecurity, fear, and difficulties in trusting. Helping adoptive parents and children deal with the feelings that accompany these losses is an important counselor role.

Each adoptive case is unique, however, and must be treated as unique by counselors and other helping service workers. The skills demanded of professionals who work with transracial adoptive families are great and include a background in both the psychological and the legal aspects of adoption. Research in the field is producing results that carry demands for a commitment to lifelong education and training by the helping service personnel who work with these diverse family situations.

Summary

Summarizing the many facets of this chapter would seem redundant. This quote from McRoy and Hall (1996) highlights many of the important issues of the diverse multiracial families discussed in this chapter:

> Children that have been placed transracially must resolve feelings about their removal from their birth families and experiences in foster care, as well as feelings about being adopted and racial identity issues resulting from transracial placement. Families must be prepared to use mental health professionals as needed to help the child address issues of grief and loss as well as adoptive and racial identity. (p. 78)

Adoptive parents also profit from work with mental health professionals to address their own as well as family issues.

5

Intervention and Treatment of Multiracial Individuals, Couples, and Families

In the first section of this chapter, current multicultural counseling competencies will be examined and discussed for their relevance to working with the multiracial population, including interracial couples, multiracial individuals, and transracially adopted persons and their families. Additional competencies that may apply specifically to this population will also be presented. The chapter will also examine each of the groups separately, and in so doing will discuss approaches, interventions, and strategies that may be effective and useful in the treatment of these groups.

Multicultural Counseling Competencies

Sue, Arredondo, and McDavis (1992) have developed standards for effective and competent multicultural counseling. The Multicultural Counseling Competencies were established to guide interpersonal counseling interactions, giving attention to culture, ethnicity, and race (Arredondo et al., 1996). At the time of their establishment, the term *multicultural,* used in the context of counseling, referred to the five major cultural groups in the United States and its territories, thus including African (Black), Asian, Caucasian (European), Latino, and Native American or indigenous groups (Arredondo et al., 1996). With the exception of Latinos, who are historically multiracial, these labels have typically been used to represent persons who declare themselves to be of monoracial backgrounds and heritage.

As discussed in Chapter 1, multiracial individuals and families threaten the traditional American way of life. The United States has relied on clear racial delineations and categories for political, social, economic, and psychological purposes and in doing so has created a negative stereotype of multiracial individuals and their families. In addition, reliance on these fixed categories has resulted in a denial of the existence of mixed-race individuals and their families. Hence, because of the negative environment that has existed until very recently, multiracial people have found it difficult to accept and to assert a multiracial identity and to develop a group consciousness (Nakashima, 1992).

Multiracial people are challenging the historical notions of race, ethnicity, culture, and community that have existed in our society, and, in doing so, they blur the boundaries between the racially stratified groups, forcing us to acknowledge the mere fact of their existence (Nakashima, 1992). According to Corey (1996), the central function of the counseling process is helping clients to recognize their own strengths, discover what is preventing them from using their strengths, and clarify what kind of person they want to be. The recognition and acceptance of one's identity can certainly be looked on as a strength; hence, if we as counselors are about helping clients to cultivate such strengths, then as a profession we must begin to look at our own acceptance of the existence of multiracial identity.

The objectives of the Multicultural Counseling Competencies require that counselors be aware of their own cultural values and biases, be aware of the client's worldview, and develop culturally appropriate intervention strategies. The dimensions of competency consist of three areas: beliefs and attitudes, knowledge, and skill (Sue, Arredondo, & McDavis, 1992). Hence, in the articulation of each of the three objectives, guidelines are given relative to each of the three dimensions. Although the competencies were initially established with the visible racial ethnic minority groups (VREG) in mind (Helms, 1990; Sue, Arredondo, & McDavis, 1992), as they are currently written they appear to give recognition to the fact that race, culture, and ethnicity are aspects of all of us and are not limited to "minorities" (Sue & Sue, 1990). Hence, in a review of the competencies in the current form, we find that they are quite applicable to the multiracial population.

A major reference tool used to operationalize the Multicultural Counseling Competencies is the Dimensions of Personal Identity Model (Arredondo & Glauner, 1992). According to Arredondo et al. (1996), the purpose of the Dimensions of Personal Identity Model is to demonstrate the complexity and holism of individuals. The model further serves as a descriptor for the examination of individual differences and shared identity based on elements that fall under the three dimensions delineated in the model. The model suggests that we are all multicultural beings; that we all possess a personal, political, and historical culture; that we are all affected by sociocultural, political, environmental, and historical events; and that multiculturalism is intertwined with numerous elements of diversity (Arredondo et al., 1996). Hays (1996b) supports this and suggests that in becoming more culturally responsive, therapists need to consider the following influences: age, development, disability, religion, ethnicity, social status, sexual orientation, indigenous heritage, national origin, and gender. In both of these models, we find support for the concept of multiracial and multiethnic identity. In viewing individuals who identify themselves as multiracial in this context, we are giving recognition to *all* of who they are.

As Wehrly (1996) points out, counselors working with multiracial individuals and their families must first have a positive sense of their own racial, ethnic, and cultural identity. Acceptance of the differences of others is often difficult to achieve without first having acceptance of self. In addition, counselors working with multiracial individuals and their families need to give special attention to the attitude and beliefs dimension of the competencies, particularly as it relates to the following objectives: counselor awareness of client's worldview and culturally appropriate intervention strategies. In working with interracial couples, multiracial individuals, and multiracial families, counselors must explore their own personal attitudes and beliefs. Hays (1996b) recommends the assessment of one's own areas of bias, ignorance, and inexperience as well. As indicated in Chapter 2, counselors working with interracial couples often make assumptions based on the myths and stereotypes that have long followed these unions. Similarly, and as addressed in Chapters 3 and 4, counselors and human service professionals have held false assumptions about multiracial individuals and about transracial adoptions.

In working with the multiracial population, a counselor is often faced with the issue of navigating within multiple racial, ethnic, and cultural milieus. For example, when White counselors work with interracial couples in which one partner is Latino and the other partner is Black, counselors may find themselves having to assess their emotional responses and reactions toward both of the racial and ethnic groups that this couple represent, as well as assessing the stereotypes and preconceived notions that they have toward individuals of both of these groups. In addition, counselors must also assess their stereotypes and preconceived notions about intermarriage. Because of the values and labels our society has placed on racial categories and the perceptions that one group is better or worse than another, it is possible that a counselor working with a Black-Latino couple or a multiracial individual of Asian-Black heritage may also need to examine the extent to which his or her stereotypical beliefs regarding racial and ethnic mixing are biased.

With respect to the attitudes and beliefs dimension relative to the objective of culturally appropriate intervention strategies, counselors who work with the multiracial and multiethnic population will often find themselves needing to work within the guise of several different religious orientations and beliefs, viewpoints on helping practices, and languages. In so doing, it is necessary to be respectful, again, of the multiple values that may be present by virtue of the multiple backgrounds represented.

The knowledge dimension of the counselor awareness of the client's worldview and the culturally appropriate intervention strategies objectives presents a challenge for counselors working with the multiracial population. In meeting both of these competency objectives, counselors are called on to be knowledgeable about all of the various groups that may be a part of a multiracial person's heritage. There is an array of sources available to counselors for this purpose. It may also be important for the counselor to have an understanding of the relationships that may exist historically between these groups as they have interacted with each other and how this history affects current-day interactions and relationships. Finally, it is important for the counselor to understand and be knowledgeable about multiracialism. In essence, the counselor must be knowledgeable about the history of racial and ethnic mixing in this country and how this history influences current-day issues affecting interracial couples, multiracial individuals, and multiracial families. The history, as attested to in Chapter 1 of this book, is important to the understanding of the legacy of the multiracial population and how the population has come to identify itself.

An additional challenge for counselors with regard to intervention strategies with this population is that of finding intervention strategies that take into account the multiplicity of cultures that may be at work in dealing with an individual, couple, or family. In working with a family, for example, where there may be an adoptive child of Asian-Indian background and an adoptive child of African American background being raised by White parents who have a biologically born White child, a knowledgeable counselor needs to understand the dynamics that may be inherent in the family by virtue of the multiple cultures. In addition, the counselor must understand how the multiple cultures affect the family structure and well-being. It is also important for the counselor to be knowledgeable about models of racial and cultural identity development. In the case of the above family, in which there are several different cultures involved, the counselor needs to be knowledgeable about how the family structure can best meet the cultural identity development needs of all involved.

The skills dimension of the counselor awareness of client's worldview objective takes the knowledge dimension a step further by suggesting that counselors familiarize themselves with research findings and information relative to the mental health issues of the population being addressed (Arredondo et al., 1996). The multiracial population is a new population of study. It is only in recent years that individuals in the social and behavioral science fields have explored the issues and concerns of this population from a healthy perspective. Many who have conducted recent research and written articles and/or books are themselves a part of the multiracial population. The lack of professional literature on this topic appears to have been another indication of the attempts to ignore and deny the validity and reality of this population's existence. As the various groups represented in the multiracial population continue to increase, the necessity also increases for counselors to seek more opportunities to enrich their knowledge and understanding of these groups to enhance their effectiveness with these groups.

The notion of counselors becoming involved with groups of people outside the context of the counseling setting is a new one. However, it is important to remember that our clients do not exist in or live in a "vacuum." There is much to be learned about individuals and groups of people simply through our involvement and connection with them in a social context. The multiracial population has been the subject of considerable social and political upheaval, particularly as it has attempted to attain a positive identity. A counselor's knowledge of how the social and political arena's acceptance of this identity has affected a multiracial individual may be useful in the development of an effective treatment intervention. Hence, knowledge of this group from a global perspective is salient.

During the administration of Dr. Courtland Lee (President, ACA, 1997-1998), members of the American Counseling Association were called to take social action. Dr. Loretta Bradley's administration (President, 1998-1999) has called on those of us in the profession to be advocates for change. During the last 10 years, a movement has begun among people of multiracial backgrounds and their supporters that defines and asserts multiracialism through political and social activism and other venues (Nakashima, 1992). The authors of this book are not suggesting that counselors become politicians, simply that we allow ourselves to become knowledgeable and aware of the issues affecting the identity of this population and, in so doing, that we be a voice of support. In advocating for the multiracial population, we can provide the psychological validation and empowerment necessary to maintain the efforts of the multiracial movement.

Finally, in looking at the skill dimension in the context of culturally appropriate intervention strategies, it is important to note the significance of the fact that the multiracial individual may, for example, be experiencing difficulties that are the manifestation of the complexities existing between and among several cultures. In this vein, the counselor cannot separate out or ignore one aspect of the individual's cultural being for another. Consultation on a variety of levels may be warranted and may involve discussion with members of multiracial support groups. Counselors who truly want to be competent and effective with the multiracial population may find themselves not only doing additional reading but also conducting empirical research that may be useful in view of the fact that the counseling professions' experience with this population is relatively new.

Approaches, Interventions, and Strategies
for Counseling Interracial Couples

It is absolutely essential that counselors who work with interracial couples examine and explore their own attitudes and beliefs about interracial relationships. Myths and stereotypes continue to cloud societal images of individuals who marry persons of another race. The counselor's awareness of his or her own attitudes and beliefs is salient to competent and effective counseling with interracial couples (Solsberry, 1994). It is crucial that counseling professionals not only be aware of personal bias but be aware of the negative effects that such bias can potentially have on the counseling process (McRoy & Freeman, 1986).

According to McRoy and Freeman (1986), biases often become apparent when counselors overemphasize the racial backgrounds of clients or deny that race is an issue at all. Further, counselors who focus excessively on cultural characteristics and differences run the risk of losing sight of their clients as individuals (Sue & Sue, 1990). Continuous monitoring of biased attitudes and beliefs by the counselor can reduce the potential of negative effects on the counseling process (Solsberry, 1994).

The myths and stereotypes about interracial marriage also have the potential to have a negative impact on the interracial couple's relationship. These myths and stereotypes are often at the root of the opposition that interracial couples experience from family and friends and may result in rejection and alienation by family and friends. Davidson (1992) suggests that counselors be critically aware of these theories and myths, recognizing their inherent racial bias and guarding against their influence in the counseling process. Couples may enter counseling in an attempt to discuss and understand the objections to their relationship (Wehrly, 1996). In recognizing the racial bias associated with the myths and objections, the counselor must be able to empathize with the couple and validate the feelings that the partners may be experiencing. It is also necessary to refocus the couple's attention to the strengths of the relationship. A major strength that is often overlooked or minimized is the ability of some couples to transcend racial bias and appreciate their vast differences. Finally, the counselor should assist the couple in recognizing and drawing strength from the partners' similarities (Davidson, 1992). In essence, the counselor must use the strength of the individual partners and the strength of the relationship to empower the couple.

It is certainly possible that a person has married an individual of another race for ulterior motives and in so doing is fulfilling the stereotypes and myths. If, in the context of the counseling process, this is revealed, it should be explored, and the counselor should assist the couple in identifying and clarifying the partners' reasons for being together. In addition, the counseling professional should assist the couple in understanding the meaning these reasons have for each partner and assist each partner in normalizing these reasons. Attempts should be made to help the couple determine if, because of love or other positive factors, the relationship has a viable chance of survival (Davidson, 1992; Okun, 1996).

Davidson (1992) suggests that in some cases a clinical professional may work with the couple and family members (if they are still around) to determine who owns which part of the problem about the interracial marriage. Family members may have to examine whether their accusations about ulterior motives expose their racism rather than indicating weakness in the couple's decision to marry. In general, interracial marriages and partnerships still present concern for members of our society. In working with couples and their families, it is important for the counselor to help them become aware that in accepting the relationship, they may be dealing on a higher moral level than some of their friends and associates. This may carry some high demands (Davidson, 1992), including that of role modeling what it means to live harmoniously in a multicultural society.

According to Solsberry (1994), the mental health counselor who works with an interracially married client of the same race as the mental health counselor may assume that no intercultural issue exists between the counselor and the client. The interracial marriage, however, probably places the client in a position that is culturally different from that of the mental health counselor. As indicated by Sue, Arredondo, and McDavis (1992), the culturally skilled counselor has knowledge and understanding of the life experiences, cultural heritage, and historical background of culturally different clients. However, by virtue of the influences of being married to a person of a different race and culture, the client who is of the same background as the counselor may have a very different cultural experience and worldview than the counselor. Thus, in working with this client and selecting the therapeutic approach and strategies to be used, the counselor needs to be cognizant of these issues.

It is important, when interracial couples present concerns regarding the relationship, that counselors explore the basis for and possible origins of these concerns. Ibrahim and Schroeder (1990) also suggest that an assessment be conducted to help the counselor understand each partner's worldview and cultural identity, as well as to help each partner understand the other's worldview and cultural identity. According to Okun (1996), differences in expression of emotion, expression of physical affection, beliefs of partners regarding gender roles, power distribution, cultural influences on family structure, views about parenting, and the meaning of love should be considered in any intercultural marriage. According to Ibrahim and Schroeder (1990), in addition to examining worldview and other cultural matters, the following may also be explored: the couple's satisfaction with the relationship, the effectiveness of communication between the partners, the commitment and level of solidarity in the relationship, the developmental differences that each partner has experienced or expects to experience, the occupational status of both partners, and the family role expectations of both partners. In examining concerns that may be a function of the cultural differences that exist between the partners, it is important to help couples explore the following: how each partner defines his or her cultural identity, the meaning that cultural identity has for each of them, and how the meaning given to each one's cultural identity influences and affects the relationship and the dynamics within the relationship (Okun, 1996). The exploration of each partner's worldview and cultural basis can assist the couple in understanding some of the reasons for the partners' conflicts (Ibrahim & Schroeder, 1990).

Ibrahim and Schroeder (1990) suggest the use of a psychoeducational approach in helping couples resolve cultural conflicts in their relationship. This approach teaches couples a cross-cultural communication strategy that can enhance their communication and their multicultural awareness. In addition, the intervention, which incorporates relationship enhancement therapy, bicultural effectiveness training, and curriculum to enhance multiculturalism, enhances each partner's ability to understand his or her conflicts, learn to resolve them, and learn to accept the other as a cultural being (Ibrahim & Schroeder, 1990).

As discussed in Chapter 2, the acknowledgement of racial and cultural oppression and prejudice by both members of the couple is salient. As well, both partners must be able to articulate their feelings and experiences related to oppression and prejudice and discuss the impact that these have had on their individual lives. Most important, partners must be able to articulate the impact that oppression and prejudice have had on how they view themselves, each other, and the relationship. If they are parents, they must also explore the ways in which these issues have affected how they view themselves as parents, how they view their children, and how they view their relationship with their children. As counselors, it is important that we have an understanding of the impact of social stratification, as well as the complex dynamics of privilege and oppression. We must also understand the history and sociopolitical complexities that are at the root of societal issues and concerns related to racial and ethnic mixing, as these issues most definitely affect the lives of interracial couples.

Approaches, Interventions, and Strategies for Counseling Interracial Gay and Lesbian Couples

As in the case of counseling with heterosexual interracial couples, counselors who work with gay and lesbian interracial couples should assess their own attitudes and beliefs about people who are in relationships with persons of a race or culture different from that of their own. As noted in Chapter 1, there are also myths and stereotypes about gay and lesbian people who engage in interracial relationships. Counselors need to be aware of these and evaluate themselves and their perceptions in this area. In addition, because of the complexities of this issue for lesbian interracial couples, it is important that counseling involve exploration of the partners' experience of their relationship, including their reasons for being together and their expectations about being in the relationship. Another salient issue to explore in working with lesbian couples is the presumptions each partner may have about White women and women of color (Greene, 1994a). The insight that may be gained from this exploration may be useful in addressing other dynamics and issues that may be of concern in the relationship.

In exploring the above, each partner's relationship with family of origin and sociocultural community may become apparent. Where each individual is in terms of the coming-out process may provide an additional challenge to the couple. Opposition to homosexuality is found in all segments of our society. Cultural norms regarding issues of homosexuality and sexual identity prevail (Chan, 1992; Clunis & Green, 1988; Greene, 1997; Greene & Boyd-Franklin, 1996; Gutierrez & Dworkin, 1992; Johnson & Keren, 1996; Morales, 1992; Smith, 1997; Tafoya, 1997). In African American communities, homosexuality is sometimes viewed negatively and as a product of White culture (Gutierrez & Dworkin, 1992). This sentiment may be found in other communities as well. The extent to which a partner has not come out to his or her family and cultural community, as well as the extent to which a partner is not accepted by his or her family and cultural community as a result of coming out about their homosexuality, may affect the dynamics within the couple relationship (Greene & Boyd-Franklin, 1996; Johnson & Keren, 1996; Smith, 1997). The most salient concern for some partners may be the reactions their families have, not only to their sexual identity but to the possibility of having to acknowledge an existing relationship and accept a new person into the family (Johnson & Keren, 1996; Smith, 1997). This may add to the complexity of things for gays and lesbians involved in interracial relationships and, particularly, interracial relationships between White and non-White partners. In working through this issue, counselors may first find themselves seeing each partner in the relationship separately, particularly depending upon what phase the individual or individuals are at in the coming-out process. It is important that the counselor be sensitive to the challenges inherent in this process and be supportive of both partners, recognizing that they may be at very different places in the process. The counselor might also, for example, need to be skillful at assisting one partner who may be in a waiting period, while at the same time supporting the other partner to proceed into the next phase or step of the coming-out process. In addition, the counselor will need to assist the partners in discussing their feelings with each other during this challenging time with each other, while at the same time encouraging and supporting each other. Honest, open dialogue between the partners regarding anxieties and concerns can lend to the growth and strength of the couple relationship (Greene & Boyd-Franklin, 1996; Smith, 1997).

According to Greene and Boyd-Franklin (1996), in discussing family disclosure issues with lesbian interracial couples involving a Black partner, it is important for the counselor to explore the possible responses of specific African American family members and not to accept expectations of blanket acceptance or rejection by family. However, it is also important that the counselor anticipate the possibility of negative family reactions to disclosure and coming out and prepare the couple for this possibility (Greene & Boyd-Franklin, 1996).

Smith (1997) indicates that it is important for the counselor to be mindful of the different expectations of the partners and encourage their continuing dialogue as the coming-out process is unfolding. The counselor must be mindful of the degree to which each partner identifies with his or her family and racial or cultural group and facilitate the couple's discussion of this as well. An individual who is coming out or disclosing to family is often at a very different place than family members may be. Hence, in acknowledgement of this fact, it is important that the counseling professional assist each partner in anticipating the varied responses from the family, as well as assisting each partner in developing strategies for dealing with these responses in the context of the couple relationship and strategies for supporting each other. This may be of particular importance in White and non-White interracial relationships (Greene & Boyd-Franklin, 1996; Johnson & Keren, 1996).

A treatment modality that is often recommended for one or both partners of gay and lesbian interracial relationships is a support group that focuses on issues of sexual orientation and/or culture and ethnicity (Gutierrez & Dworkin, 1992; Johnson & Keren, 1996). In addition, and as in the case of counseling with heterosexual interracial couples, strategies that include opportunities for couples to de-emphasize racial, ethnic, or cultural differences and thus emphasize the strengths and similarities that exist in the relationship help to empower both partners and thus empower the relationship (Johnson & Keren, 1996).

Approaches, Interventions, and Strategies for Counseling Multiracial Individuals

In 1990, The U.S. Census Bureau reported that approximately 2 million children under the age of 18 were of mixed heritage. As we go into the next century, this number will undoubtedly continue to increase. Multiracial individuals have historically been the subject of scrutiny because their very existence forces us to deal with significant issues related to racism and oppression in our society. Just as there have been myths and stereotypes associated with interracial coupling and marriage, myths and stereotypes abound about the offspring of these unions. Counselors working with multiracial individuals at any stage of development must examine their own attitudes and beliefs about multiracial individuals. They must also examine their own attitudes and beliefs about what it means to be an individual with more than one racial or ethnic heritage in our society. Having an understanding of this context will better assist counselors in gaining a perspective of the challenges faced by parents raising multiracial children, as well as the multiracial individuals themselves. This level of understanding may also assist counselors in better understanding the counseling needs of multiracial individuals.

The findings of a study conducted by Nishimura and Bol (1997) suggest that school counselors carry a variety of perspectives about the counseling needs of multiracial children. These perspectives, however, are sometimes based on myths, stereotypes, and other forms of misinformation and are not representative of the true needs of individual children. The development that takes place relative to a preschool- and elementary-school-age child's racial and ethnic identity has considerable impact on later stages of identity development (Brandell, 1988; McRoy & Freeman, 1986). Thus the support that a child receives that is based on myths or other forms of misinformation can have a negative impact on the development of a positive identity later in life.

Assessment of multiracial individuals who come for counseling should involve consideration of the multiracial identity development models discussed in chapter 3. In addition, Root (1994) lists these six themes around which issues and concerns arise for the multiracial individual: "(1) uniqueness, (2) acceptance and belonging, (3) physical appearance, (4) sexuality, (5) self-esteem and (6) identity" (p. 462). These are also key areas for the assessment of multiracial individuals who come for counseling. Any one of these themes may be salient to the concerns an individual may be dealing with at a particular developmental stage, but it should be mentioned that these areas are not mutually exclusive.

1. *Uniqueness.* This area interfaces with all of the other five areas. A lifetime of feeling that one is different may lead to behaviors that may be misinterpreted as pathological. In an attempt to be better understood by others, individuals who have felt misunderstood over a lifetime may have developed a style of communicating that includes much detail and an overemphasis on context. This manner of communicating may appear compulsive or even paranoid to others who do not understand the unique world in which the multiracial individual has lived.

2. *Acceptance and belonging.* A key concept in feeling that one is accepted and belongs is the feeling of being connected. Multiracial people do not fit the rigid racial labels developed by the dominant society to preserve color lines. Hence, they often do not feel connected with any group except other multiracial people. Houston (1997) describes the pain of not being

accepted fully into either the African American or Asian American communities of her racial roots. Membership in many groups may not necessarily mean that the multiracial individual feels a real connection to the people in those groups.

3. *Physical appearance.* According to Hall (1997), focus on physical features may be more common among people of mixed-race heritage because they typically have different features than those who are of one race. Physical appearance seems to be more paramount for mixed-race women than for mixed-race men. Women tend to define themselves and measure their self-worth more in terms of relationships to others than do men. Many multiracial people have experienced a lifetime of being stared at or of having a name that does not fit their physical appearance. Experiencing repeated questions about identity can lead to a feeling of always being judged and evaluated (Root, 1994). Because multiracial persons can change their physical appearances to represent different parts of their racial heritages, it is important for them to develop a consistent and strong internal identity.

4. *Sexuality.* The stereotypic myth that the multiracial female is a sexual object to be sought and dominated by males has contributed to discrimination against mixed-race women. Relationships based on this myth rarely lead to emotionally fulfilling experiences. In addition, sexual promiscuity may be strongly tied to acceptance and belonging.

5. *Self-esteem.* The multiracial individual's self-esteem interfaces with the other five themes around which issues may arise. This is especially true if the individual seems to be controlled mainly by an external frame of reference.

6. *Identity.* Having an identity includes a feeling of belonging and connectedness. The multiracial person has a multicultural heritage. Developing feelings of belonging to cultures that appear to have disparate values can be challenging. Individuals who have had positive exposure to the values and behaviors of their racial heritages develop a flexibility in affirming their identity.

The discussion of counseling interventions with multiracial individuals will be presented in four parts: counseling with multiracial preschool and elementary school children, counseling with multiracial adolescents, counseling with multiracial college students, and counseling with multiracial adults.

Counseling Multiracial Preschool and
Elementary School Children

Counselors working in school settings must take a significant role in assisting school personnel in becoming multiculturally competent and aware. This should entail mandatory training and in-service opportunities that allow all staff to examine their attitudes and beliefs about all that encompasses our multicultural society. The training should also include information on the knowledge and skills necessary for working with children and families of diverse backgrounds and orientations, particularly multiracial children and other children who are raised in multiracial family environments. In addition, they must assist school administrators and teachers in developing multicultural curriculums, programs, and services that are inclusive of multiracial issues (Derman-Sparks, 1989).

A good multicultural curriculum is one that provides multiracial children, and all other children, opportunities to see themselves as individuals made up of specific features. Through projects, cooperative learning experiences, and group process opportunities facilitated by trained school personnel, children can be taught not to look at people in a context of group labels but to look at each person as coming with a variety of different physical and cultural characteristics (Adejando-Wright, 1985; Wardle, 1992a). Of course, no school programming can be effective without providing similar programming opportunities for parents, family members, and the community at large. School counselors can explore possible resources in the community and arrange for consultative and collaborative ventures. Involvement on the part of school, family, and the community provides support, reinforcement, and empowerment for children (Gibbs & Moskowitz-Sweet, 1991).

In assessing the problems or difficulties that a multiracial pre-school or elementary school child may have, it is necessary that the counselor be able to differentiate between age- or stage-appropriate problems and concerns and those problems and concerns that may be related to the child-rearing practices of both of the parents, the parents' relationship, other familial conflicts, or racial- and ethnic-related issues and concerns (Okun, 1996). Counselors should be aware of the possibility that a child's presenting concern may be a mask for deeper racial or ethnic identity problems, but counselors should not assume that the concerns of all multiracial children are always a result of racial or ethnic identity issues (Herring, 1992).

Trust is a core dimension in the development of a positive counseling relationship. In working with a multiracial child, the development of this trust early in the counseling relationship is critical, particularly if the child has issues and concerns related to racial or ethnic factors (Gibbs, 1985; Herring, 1992; Wehrly, 1996). How the actual assessment of the problem is conducted may depend on the actual age, understanding, and cognitive processing ability of the child. The counselor would do well to approach the assessment of the problem with sensitivity (Okun, 1996; Wehrly, 1996). Moreover, and particularly in the case where it becomes clear that a child is experiencing feelings and exhibiting behaviors that are manifestations of rejection or alienation due to racial or ethnic factors, it is important that the counselor allow the child to verbalize feelings regarding his or her experiences and not invalidate these feelings (Gibbs, 1989; Sebring, 1985). At the same time, the counselor must assist children in understanding the connection between their behavior and the struggles they might be experiencing related to confusion about their mixed heritage (Sebring, 1985).

As expressed earlier, the development of a positive identity and self-concept is of paramount importance for the multiracial child. In working with multiracial children, counselors must assist them in building their self-esteem by helping them to recognize and identify their individual strengths and abilities, assisting them in developing positive alternatives for coping with conflict and supporting them in these efforts, and assisting them in developing and pursuing their own interests (Sebring, 1985). In addition, according to Herring (1992), when assisting children in forming positive feelings about all of their ethnic and cultural roots, it is important that they be encouraged to explore all sides of their racial heritage. Effective individual treatment strategies consist of bibliotherapy, role playing, journaling, and various forms of creative writing and art (Gibbs, 1989; Wehrly, 1996).

As will be discussed later in this chapter, it is always helpful for the counselor to involve parents and other siblings who may be in the child's family. The counselor's understanding of the interactions and dynamics of the family with regard to its multiracial status can provide the counselor with insight that may be useful to have in continuing to work with the child. Wehrly (1996) suggests that counselors and teachers meet with the parents of multiracial children with whom they are working to discuss issues and concerns that may be unique to their family. Counselors can encourage parents' efforts to foster their child's awareness of their varied backgrounds. The counselor's willingness to work with the family in an effort to help the child feel positive about the various aspects of his or her heritage is affirming and provides support and validation to the multiracial experience (Adler, 1987).

Counseling Multiracial Adolescents

Gibbs (1989) suggests that counselors working with multiracial adolescents assess for possible conflicts in five major psychosocial areas: multiple racial or ethnic identity, social marginality, sexuality and choice of sexual partners, separation from parents, and educational and career aspirations. Children of mixed-race backgrounds may have the additional challenges of dealing with stress and conflict related to their mixed heritage as they move toward adolescence. In working with multiracial adolescents, counselors must distinguish between typical adolescent developmental behavior and behavior that may be indicative of difficulties stemming from their multiracial heritage (Gibbs & Moskowitz-Sweet, 1991). In view of this, it has been suggested by Gibbs (1989) that the most salient factor to assess is the multiracial adolescent's attitudes regarding his or her multiracial background. Other crucial factors to be examined in the assessment process are attitudes that family members, including extended family, have concerning their multiracial status; support resources available in the school and community; and social support networks (Gibbs & Moskowitz-Sweet (1991). Pinderhughes (1995) suggests that positive individual, family, and social networks be identified to provide additional support during the therapeutic process.

With the primary developmental task of adolescence being that of achieving a firm identity (Erikson, 1963), a major hurdle for multiracial adolescents is that of blending their multiple identities into a distinct solid identity that enables them to merge positive aspects of their varied backgrounds, acknowledges their uniqueness, and encourages a strong sense of self-worth (Gibbs & Moskowitz-Sweet, 1991).

As in the case of work with younger multiracial children, school counselors must take an active part in identifying multiracial adolescents with identity-related problems, training teachers and other school personnel in the issues and concerns of multiracial adolescents and in how to effectively recognize problems and assist with problem resolution, offering programs and services for multiracial adolescents, and identifying and providing community referral options. Again, it is suggested that for treatment to be effective, counselors must work to engage the cooperation of the multiracial adolescent's family, teachers, and community (Gibbs & Moskowitz-Sweet, 1991). Therapeutic treatment with the multiracial adolescent should focus on the following: validating adolescents' feelings about their multiracial status, supporting their development of a positive self-concept, assisting them in understanding the connection between problematic behaviors and difficulties they may be experiencing concerning their mixed heritage, and assisting them in the exploration of all aspects of their backgrounds in an effort to build and strengthen a positive self-image (Pinderhughes, 1995).

Counseling adolescents requires that the practitioner first be able to develop a close working alliance with the youth. In working with the multiracial teen, care should be taken to provide multiculturally sensitive intervention (Gibbs, 1985). According to Gibbs and Moskowitz-Sweet (1991), treatment strategies should take into account the adolescent's ego strength and development and focus on the enhancement of skills in the areas of problem solving, values clarification, decision making, and goal setting. According to Pinderhughes (1995), specific treatment strategies include focused discussions, bibliotherapy, and homework assignments, all geared toward exploration of issues of racial identity and the development of a positive self-concept related to one's racial identity. Other specific strategies include role plays, journaling, storytelling, and a variety of behavioral goal-setting techniques. Additional interventions that can be used in the school setting are peer support groups and peer counseling (Gibbs & Moskowitz-Sweet, 1991).

Counseling Multiracial College Students

The traditional-age college student is an individual who (in a developmental context) is moving out of adolescence into young adulthood. As we have observed the young men and women with whom we have worked over the years, we have witnessed changes that seem to suggest that adolescence often gets prolonged during the college years, and the search for a solid identity continues sometimes long after the student has graduated. Hence, many of the strategies that were recommended in terms of individual treatment for multiracial adolescents may also be useful in work with multiracial college students. However, the college student's movement toward emancipation from family should not be forgotten. Involvement with peers and social networks were important throughout adolescence, and these relationships often take on an even greater meaning in college by providing the supportive roles once filled by siblings and parents. Nishimura (1998) has discussed the role that college counselors and other student services personnel must take in addressing the concerns of multiracial college students. She first emphasizes the necessity of campus personnel's recognizing this ever-growing segment of our population and developing strategies for confronting the challenges it presents.

Most college campuses today offer sponsored groups and activities for students of color. These can include Latino student organizations, Black student unions, Asian student groups, and international student organizations. Groups specifically for multiracial students are not always available. The struggle to discover where they "fit in" racially is a common one for multiracial college students (Grove, 1991). Often, multiracial students find themselves attempting to fit in with the monoracially focused campus groups and organizations and, yet, in doing so, find that they are not accepted. This lack of acceptance is generally based on reactions to their physical appearance and questions that are raised about who or what they are (Grove, 1991). Feelings of loss, isolation, and confusion can occur for those students whose identity formation is not yet complete, particularly if they feel forced to negate aspects of themselves (McRoy & Freeman, 1986; Sebring, 1985).

College counselors must take the responsibility of becoming more aware themselves of the ever-growing multiracial population and its needs and concerns. In doing so, however, counselors must also examine their own personal attitudes and beliefs about persons of mixed race and their families. Moreover, they must take the lead in bringing the issues and concerns of the multiracial population to the awareness of faculty, staff, administrators, and student leaders. This can be accomplished through advocating for training workshops, guest lecture series, and cultural activities, all geared toward the recognition and enhancement of multicultural education and understanding that is inclusive of all (Nishimura, 1998). Counselors can support the establishment of a support group for multiracial students. As suggested by Nishimura (1998), a support group can positively acknowledge the diversity of the campus community while at the same time acknowledging the diversity found in our society. Multiracial students involved in such groups can use the group to gain strength and affirmation as they navigate the campus environment. Alipuria (1990) stressed the importance that "community" has in the development of positive identity for multiracial individuals. The development of a support group for multiracial college students can provide a sense of community and thus have a positive impact on self-esteem and identity.

Multiracial students seek the services of campus counseling centers for a variety of reasons. Certainly college counselors need to be aware that students of multiracial backgrounds may present issues related to the concerns or difficulties they may be experiencing by virtue of their mixed heritage, but, like other students, they may well present with the same basic developmental issues and concerns faced by students of all backgrounds. Hence, the warning—that counselors need not make assumptions that every multiracial student has problems related to his or her multiracial identity

(Grove, 1991; Nishimura, 1998). Concerns that are related to the student's multiracial identity should be addressed with sensitivity.

Counseling Multiracial Adults

Although it is suggested by Root (1994) that multiracial men and women seldom enter counseling with the goal of resolving overt issues concerning their multiracial identity, counseling professionals need to be aware of the potential impact that being of mixed heritage may have on one's life. Logan, Freeman, and McRoy (1987) recommend the use of an ecological approach in the assessment and treatment of issues presented by multiracial adults. This approach can be used to help the client and counselor determine the prevalence of racial and cultural identity concerns. The ecological approach uses the genogram, ecomap, and cultural continuum to help individuals to clarify what it means for them to identify themselves multiracially (Logan, Freeman, & McRoy, 1987). The genogram is used to explore family relationships and dynamics, roles, and significant life events. With multiracial individuals, it is suggested that the genogram be taken a step further, to explore the racial and ethnic heritage of family members, the attitudes of immediate and extended family related to the existence of people with multiple heritages in the family, and the level of functioning in family relationships. The relationships that the individual and his or her family have had with networks, including neighborhood, schools, local community, and institutions within the community related to their multiple heritages, may also be explored. Details related to the individual and his or her family's basic development and lifestyle may be discussed, as they may also have relevance to the client's multiracial identity and backgrounds (Logan et al., 1987).

The ecomap is similar to the genogram in that it uses the same connecting lines and symbols to signify relationships. The multiracial individual's family is depicted in a large circle, around which smaller circles signifying connections with other family and social support networks are drawn. The individual and family's relationships to other family and social support networks are gleaned through the use of connecting lines. The ecomap can be used to explore and discuss the client and his or her family's relationship with external networks. The extent to which the individual has had positive or negative experiences with these networks can provide insight regarding where and who the individual can rely on for empowerment and support and how he or she may need to re-evaluate and reframe relationships (Logan et al., 1987).

The cultural continuum can be used to help multiracial persons explore patterns of adaptation to circumstances in their lives that are related to their mixed racial heritage while at the same time examining the consequences and outcomes of previous and current choices made in dealing with their backgrounds and various circumstances. The potentials and possibilities of future choices may also be examined. The continuum consists of four cultural classifications or responses, including denial of cultural or racial significance, assimilation with the dominant culture or race, assimilation with the minority culture or race, or multiracial identification. Advantages and disadvantages are provided for each response category (Logan et al., 1987).

Root (1994) recommends that counseling professionals be aware of the six general themes that are related to being multiracial in developing strategies for counseling multiracial adults. These themes (uniqueness, acceptance and belonging, physical appearance, sexuality, self-esteem, and identity), which were presented earlier in this chapter, provide a useful context for understanding the issues and concerns that multiracial adults may present. According to Root (1994), these themes are important to consider because of their possible relevance to the multiracial adult's interpersonal style, perception of the environment, and manifestations of distress. Further, the adult's geographical location, degree of contact with other multiracial individuals, and the degree to which family has provided the individual with support, preparation, and validation for a multiracial existence will determine the prevalence of these issues for the individual during the course of the lifespan (Root, 1992). The extent to which the counselor is able to understand the issues underlying the themes will determine his or her ability to facilitate the relief of symptoms and develop strategies for effective problem solving and intervention (Root, 1994).

The recommendations of Root (1994) and Logan et al. (1987) require the counselor to give consideration to societal forces that have affected the multiracial adult. Tangible strategies that may be used in the process of counseling multiracial adults include homework assignments and bibliotherapy.

Approaches, Interventions, and Strategies
for Counseling Multiracial Families

As indicated by Wehrly (1996), multiracial families develop in a variety of ways: through interracial marriage and cohabitation, through transracial adoption, through transracial foster care, and through transracial single parenting. Our discussion of counseling multiracial families will focus on those that have developed through interracial marriage and cohabitation, as well as through transracial adoption. Counselors working with multiracial families may find that they present with a variety of unique circumstances (Root, 1992). Moreover, counselors working with these families may focus on issues not typically addressed in monoracial families. It is important to make clear here that being a multiracial family does not imply pathology or psychological dysfunction. However, it is necessary to acknowledge that multiracial families may have more issues to deal in relation to their multiple cultural identities, competing loyalties, and the confusing messages of a still racist society (Okun, 1996).

Assessment with multiracial families may include several steps. Faulkner and Kich (1983) suggest examining the family with respect to its functioning in three areas: family life cycle, intimacy and boundaries, and children's responses. They further suggest that exploration of one of these may provide insight with regard to functioning in the other areas. Key family life cycle events include courtship, engagement, and marriage of the couple; birth of first child; sharing of influence with other authorities when the child begins school; emergence of adolescence; launching of offspring; the middle years of the family; the aging family. The manner in which these life cycle events are dealt with may be influenced by the differences in the racial and cultural backgrounds of the parents (Faulkner & Kich, 1983).

The assessment of intimacy and boundaries entails examination of the extent to which the varied cultural backgrounds of the couple affect communication, decision making, negotiation of problems, and management of stress and disagreement within the family. Assessment in this area may also involve examining how the family manages external forces that may result in stress. The area of the assessment process that deals with children's responses entails an exploration of the children's experiences related to their mixed racial heritage. In this exploratory process, the counselor may examine the manner in which parents have responded to the racial or cultural identity problems or concerns experienced by their children, as well as how the parents have resolved their own individual racial and cultural identity issues (Faulkner & Kich, 1983).

Okun (1996) further suggests that, in meeting with families who are dealing with child-related concerns, appropriate assessment may include examining the extent to which the difficulties are related to developmental factors, deficiencies or inadequacies in parenting skills, marital or relationship conflicts in the home environment, academic difficulties, or racial- and ethnic-related difficulties.

Okun (1996) emphasized that treatment is not likely to have much impact if the therapeutic climate and the attitude and skills of the practitioner are perceived as unaccepting and biased. Hence, practitioners must examine the context in which they view interracial couples and their offspring, as well as look at their views on transracial adoption and foster care. Because (for example in meeting with the family) the counselor will find him- or herself dealing with people of two or three different racial and cultural groups, the therapeutic strategies employed will need to be considerate of the varied worldviews and perspectives out of which each person operates (Wehrly, 1996). Faulkner and Kich (1983) recommended the use of four techniques that counselors can use in the process of building a strong therapeutic relationship with a multiracial family: joining and disclosure, clarification of questions, family self-identification, and hierarchy and culture.

Joining and disclosure techniques are used to build the therapeutic relationship with the family. Joining entails creating a bond between therapist and family; disclosure, used appropriately, entails the therapist's further solidifying the bond through the sharing of information that might assist all family members in feeling that the therapist shares some connection to them. In providing clarification of questions, the counselor explains to the family the purpose or motive for asking specific questions, particularly those with a racial or cultural focus. The family self-identification process involves examining how the family responds to questions of how they as a group identify themselves to each other and to the world. The data obtained from their responses provide insight regarding how the family views itself from a racial and cultural perspective and how it has responded to situations that have invalidated or negated aspects of its multiracial heritage. Hierarchy and culture require the counselor to have understanding and competence with regard to family dynamics and roles and the impact of culture on family dynamics, roles, and interactions. The counselor's insights regarding hierarchy and culture will be useful in understanding how to effectively work with the family (Faulkner & Kich, 1983).

Actual therapeutic intervention with multiracial families will vary depending on the issues and needs of the family members. However, whether the intervention is primary, consisting of psychoeducationally oriented tasks and activities, or secondary, consisting of intensive counseling and psychotherapy (Ibrahim, 1998), general systems theory is useful to apply. Looking first at secondary intervention, Kahn (1993) recommended the use of the therapeutic concepts of the structural family therapy approach, the extended family systems paradigm, and the experiential family systems therapy in transcultural family therapy. Wehrly (1996) suggests that modifications of both the structural family therapy approach and the extended family systems paradigm are appropriate to use with multiracial families.

Ibrahim (1998) states that primary intervention must take place in the home, the schools, and the community and involve educating parents, teachers, school personnel, community agency personnel, recreation groups and leagues, coaches, and others about the issues and challenges faced by multiracial youngsters. The major focus of primary intervention should be that of empowerment. Gibbs and Moskowitz-Sweet (1991) recommend total family involvement in activities geared toward enhancing the self-esteem of children and enhancing family pride. These activities include ethnic and cultural activities and multiracial or multicultural social activities. Engaging in church-based activities that provide a spiritual component to cultural enrichment, and politically oriented activities geared toward improvement of the social climate for multiracial individuals and families, are also recommended. Grosz (1989) made note of the more than 30 support groups and organizations that currently exist across the United States to assist multiracial individuals and their families in affirming their heritages.

Special Issues in Counseling With Families That Have Become Multiracial Through Transracial Adoption or Foster Care

It is important to begin by emphasizing that although it should not be assumed that the presenting concerns of the transracial adoptive or foster care family are due to adoption, foster care, or multiraciality, the assessment process may at some point involve determining the extent to which these may be contributing factors (Okun, 1996). The counseling assessment process may involve observation of the manner in which the family attends to or addresses the issues of adoption or foster care and the obvious racial and cultural differences. In situations where the family may not be open about these matters, sensitivity will have to be employed in the timing and the manner in which the clinician probes for information. Determining the level of support, acceptance, and dynamics of relationships with extended family members may also be important, as will determining the extent to which the family avails itself of other support resources and networks, including those which may be available in the school district, church, or community (Okun, 1996).

Counseling intervention for problems that may be related to issues of adoption and foster care and racial and cultural issues will vary depending upon who in the family has ownership of the problems. For example, if it is determined that the adopted or foster care child is the one struggling, counseling intervention will have to be based on the developmental phase or stage of the child, both at the time of entry into the family and at the time of treatment. Expressive therapies, including play therapy and art therapy, may be helpful to use with young children who may be dealing with feelings related to adoption and race or culture (Okun, 1996).

If there are biological children in the family and it is determined that they are experiencing difficulties, therapeutic intervention will need to consider the biological children's developmental phase or stage, both at the time of the adopted or foster child's entry into the home and at the time of treatment. Parents will need to be taught to be sensitive and empathic to the concerns and needs of biological children so that these may be dealt with openly. Whether the adopted child is from abroad or from the United States will also present some implications for therapeutic intervention and treatment. For example, with children adopted from abroad at a later age, issues related to language, rituals, and customs that the child may already be familiar with will need to be considered when deciding on methods of intervention (Okun, 1996).

Whatever approach is taken, the counselor must ensure a safe environment that allows family members to express their feelings and concerns openly. Here too, the counselor must be willing to assess his or her own views in relation to transracial adoption and foster care. As in working with other multiracial families, the counselor must be knowledgeable about community resources that provide support and validation to the multiplicity of backgrounds that may exist in transracial adoptive and foster care families.

The fact that gay and lesbian individuals and couples are taking part in transracial adoptions and foster care arrangements was discussed in chapter 4. It is necessary to mention here again that the counseling literature presents virtually no information on this population, and much less on treatment and intervention with this population. It is our position that counselors working with gay and lesbian transracial adoptive and foster care families should follow the same recommendations that have been provided for counseling other transracial adoptive and foster care families—keeping in mind, however, the additional challenges gay and lesbian families may face that are related to our homophobic society. First and foremost, in working with gay and lesbian transracial adoptive and foster care families, the counselor will need to assess his or her own attitudes and beliefs regarding issues of homosexuality, transracial adoption and foster care, and gay and lesbian families.

According to Okun (1996), in working with gay and lesbian families, the validating, supportive style of the counselor is the most significant component of effective treatment, more than the use of a particular model or strategy. As mentioned earlier, components of primary prevention are always helpful in working with families. With gay and lesbian transracial adoptive and foster care families, the counselor will need to be knowledgeable about resources that may be available to provide additional information, support, assistance, and affirmation specific to the issues of these families.

We are being called upon by our profession to be multiculturally competent. As discussed by Sue et al. (1998), multicultural counseling competence requires us to expand and take on alternative helping roles, which include adviser, advocate, consultant, change agent, facilitator of indigenous support systems, and facilitator of indigenous healing systems. In exploring the various concerns, issues, and challenges of the multiracial population, what has become clear is the role that members of our profession must take in addressing this population. As Oriti, Bibb, and Mahboubi (1996) suggest, the particular therapeutic approach or strategy to be employed may not be as important a consideration in working with the multiracial population as is the extent to which we provide services that are accepting and appreciative of the diverse heritages, orientations, and worldviews of this population. Our work with this population may require an incorporation of political processes as we begin to understand the role that oppression has played in the challenges faced by this population and as we begin our work as advocates and change agents.

Summary

This chapter has examined and discussed the current multicultural counseling competencies and the relevance these have to counseling the multiracial population. Approaches, interventions, and strategies that may be useful in the treatment of the multiracial population were presented.

6

―――――
―――――
―――

Case Studies

This chapter is a presentation of case studies used to provide examples of some of the challenges faced by the multiracial population and how these challenges can be assessed and effectively dealt with in counseling practice. The case studies include discussions of

1. counselor roles in work with preschool and elementary children in multiracial families,
2. counselor roles in work with a transracially adopted college student,
3. counselor roles in work with multiracial adults,
4. counselor roles in work with a multiracial couple, and
5. counselor roles in work with a gay multiracial family.

Counselor Roles in Work With Preschool and Elementary Children in Multiracial Families[1]

As noted in the preceding chapters, multiracial children are subject to stares, statements, and questions from people who notice their different appearance. The way multiracial children respond to this intrusion in their lives will be heavily influenced by how the family and other significant people in their lives have prepared these children for living with their multiracial identities.

Case Example

Joe is a 10-year-old biracial Black-White fourth grader whose family moved to the Thomas Jefferson Elementary School District during the summer. Early in the school year, Joe is referred to Mrs. Jones, the elementary school counselor at Thomas Jefferson School, because of fighting on the playground and lack of participation in classroom activities.

Thomas Jefferson School is located in an upper middle class suburb of a large city. The student population is largely White with a small minority of Asian American and African American students. There are no other biracial fourth graders at the school. The administrative, teaching, and support personnel of the school are representative of the diversity of the nearby urban area.

Joe's mother is White and is a lawyer with a large downtown corporation. Joe's father is Black and is a surgeon at the nearby area hospital. Joe's parents work long hours at their respective jobs. An older brother is in high school and is an avid sports participant. Joe participates in an after-school program sponsored by the local YMCA. His older brother picks Joe up after football practice and is in charge of Joe until their parents arrive home from work.

In the first interview with Joe, Mrs. Jones learns that Joe feels homesick for his old school and the friends he had there. Joe tells Mrs. Jones that on the playground, some of the other kids made fun of his kinky hair and tan skin. They asked him, "What are you, anyway?" Before Joe could answer, another boy called him the "N" word. This made Joe angry enough to fight the boy who called him the "N" word. Joe says he is embarrassed about fighting the boy and hopes Mrs. Jones will not tell his parents about the playground incident.

When Mrs. Jones asks Joe what is happening in his fourth grade classroom, Joe says the kids ignore him and he does not feel comfortable enough to volunteer in classroom discussions. The school records that were transferred from Joe's former school indicate that he was a very good student through Grade 3.

Counselor Roles in Work With School Personnel and Students

The administrators, counselors, faculty, and other staff of preschool and elementary schools play a significant role in helping multiracial children develop positive feelings about their racial heritages (Wardle, 1990, 1992a, 1993). Counselors can play a leading role in helping to create a climate that celebrates the diversity and dignity of all children and their families.

It is important that the counselor establish a positive working relationship with all of the people who work at the schools. One of the first steps in establishing this relationship requires counselors to get out of their offices and interact with children and all school personnel. Mrs. Jones makes it a point to be in the hall to interact with the elementary students and the school personnel before and after school. During the lunch period, she sometimes has children bring their lunch to her office and meets with them over lunch. At other times, Mrs. Jones eats lunch with the teachers or in the cafeteria with students.

Counselors model a respect for individual differences and work with the rest of the school personnel to see that individual differences are validated, enjoyed, and celebrated. Mrs. Jones models respect for the diversity at Thomas Jefferson School through her daily interactions. She has been instrumental in helping to celebrate individual differences at Thomas Jefferson School through arranging for pictures of all people who work at the school to be displayed on a bulletin board near the central office and through having class pictures mounted on the walls beside the respective classroom doors (Wardle, 1992a, 1993).

Establishing a positive working relationship with teachers may involve (a) consulting with teachers about the needs of students, (b) working with teachers in in-service training, (c) assisting with in-classroom guidance activities, and (d) helping with parent conferences.

Mrs. Jones met with Joe's teacher when the teacher referred Joe for counseling. She will continue to meet with Joe's teacher, but she will be careful to reveal confidential information only with Joe's permission. An important in-service topic for counselors to address is the process of helping all children develop positive feelings about their racial identities. Teachers at Thomas Jefferson realize that they know little about the process of children's racial identity development, especially the process of racial identity development for children with more than one racial heritage.

Because Mrs. Jones presented a workshop in which teachers investigated their own racial and ethnic heritages the previous year, she believes they are ready for an in-service workshop on helping students explore their racial backgrounds. At the close of last year's workshop, several of the teachers indicated that they were going to help their own children explore family histories over the summer.

At the request of the teachers, Mrs. Jones will present an in-service workshop that will include background information on children's development of racial identities and suggested activities to help all children develop pride in their racial heritage(s). One section of the workshop will address the developmental process that multiracial children experience, including the difficult periods when children experience ambivalence toward their racial heritages and stages where they distort colors. Prejudice prevention activities will also be outlined.

Teachers are looking for materials to incorporate multiculturalism and diversity in classroom lessons and ways to help the children develop family trees. Two possible sources of information on developing family trees are *Do People Grow on Family Trees? Genealogy for Kids & Other Beginners* (Wolfman, 1991), and *"Are Those Kids Yours?"—American Families with Children Adopted from Other Countries* (Register, 1990). *Teaching Tolerance,* a free magazine that contains a wealth of stories and ideas for promoting multiculturalism and diversity in the schools, is available to teachers. It is published twice yearly by the Southern Poverty Law Center, 400 Washington Ave., Montgomery, AL 36104.

Parental cooperation will be enlisted through an article in the school newsletter that explains the class projects. The article will also talk about the role of racial and ethnic pride in the development of children's positive self-concepts. Parents will be encouraged to talk with Mrs. Jones or the school principal if they have concerns about having their children study their family's history.

One specific technique that Mrs. Jones will suggest for classroom developmental multicultural guidance is bibliotherapy, the use of books for developmental or therapeutic purposes (Wehrly, 1996, 1998). The use of books to help interracial children have vicarious cross-cultural experiences may be particularly important for interracial children like Joe who live in ethnically isolated areas and who have limited opportunities to experience multicultural environments (Ponterotto, 1991). Gay's 1987 book, *The Rainbow Effect: Interracial Families,* is one book that will be used to tell the stories of mixed-race families. Books can also help other students at Thomas Jefferson broaden their worldviews on diversity.

Mrs. Jones will work with teachers in locating resources listing multicultural and interracial books for children (Camarata, 1991; "Enriching classroom diversity," 1993; Helbig & Perkins, 1994; Horning, 1993; Kezwer, 1995; Kruse, 1992; Roberts & Cecil, 1993; Wehrly, 1996). Annotations on many interracial books are noted in volumes of *The Bookfinder* (Dreyer, 1977, 1981, 1985, 1989, 1994) and in Wehrly (1996).

Multicultural and interracial books are also included in Miller-Lachmann's (1992) *Our Family, Our Friends, Our World: An Annotated Guide to Significant Multicultural Books for Children and Teenagers*. Miller-Lachmann presents a rationale for including multicultural books from all areas of the world in the curriculum. A unique feature of the book is that it notes instances of biases and inaccuracies in the multicultural books. This information can be used to help readers "learn to read critically and to look behind stereotypes to the richness, diversity, and universal elements of each culture" (Miller-Lachmann, 1992, p. xi). A bright student like Joe may enjoy the challenge of reading critically.

Use of books for bibliotherapy will be most effective if the preschool or early elementary teacher and Mrs. Jones plan together to select the books, introduce the stories, and carry out follow-up activities. Some counselors tape-record the stories so that they can show the book's pictures and watch the nonverbal reactions of the child or children listening to the story and viewing the pictures. The tape can be turned off for discussion at appropriate times. Hearing the stories and seeing the pictures can help young interracial children realize that other boys and girls live in families like theirs where the mother and father are of different racial heritages.

The story content and the reader can also help the listeners realize that the characters in the story may be facing mixed feelings about their interracial heritage. Children are encouraged to verbalize feelings about their unique family situations. The counselor can help to validate these feelings as "OK" and assist children in learning the difference between having feelings and acting negatively on feelings. Children can also be introduced to various labels that families in the stories give to their multiracial situations. Discussion of some of the various labels used by mixed-race families can follow. This can help children with more than one racial heritage to move through Jacobs's second stage of interracial identity development, Post-Color Constancy, Biracial Label, and Racial Ambivalence.

Other activities, such as writing a different ending to the story, can be added to the use of bibliotherapy with cognitively more mature children, like Joe, who can read the stories on their own. Careful choice of appropriate stories to meet the needs of the children and timing of the reading of the stories are important early steps. The choice of follow-up activities is especially important in increasing the effectiveness of bibliotherapy. Some follow-up activities might include (a) use of open-ended questions related to the content of the story and about the feelings of the characters in the story, (b) discussions about times when the listeners or readers related to the feelings of the children in the story, (c) completion of unfinished sentences, (d) role playing of segments of the story with discussion of feelings experienced while role playing, (e) participation in art activities, and (f) formulation and discussion of different ends to the story (Cornett & Cornett, 1980).

Rosenberg's (1986) photoessay *Living in Two Worlds* will be presented for possible use for classroom bibliotherapy in all of the fourth grades at Thomas Jefferson School. In this story, people in four interracial families tell the advantages and challenges of growing up in mixed-heritage families. Children are introduced to the way these families celebrate differences in languages, religions, food, clothes, and cultural traditions. The interracial children in *Living in Two Worlds* speak of how they feel when insensitive questions or remarks are made to them. Another book, *Trevor's Story* (Kandel, 1997), is appropriate for classroom use and for Joe to read and discuss with Mrs. Jones on an individual basis. For teachers interested in developing multicultural classroom guidance units, a host of suggestions is now available in books and journals, for example: Coelho (1994) D'Andrea and Daniels (1996), Gura (1994), Hayes (1996), Henderson (1990), and Omizo and D'Andrea (1995).

Mrs. Jones is also prepared to facilitate in-service training on culturally sensitive active listening. Faculty and staff who have already experienced this training will be invited to serve as cofacilitators for the in-service workshop. Learning and practicing the skills of culturally sensitive active listening can greatly magnify positive working relationships throughout the school and can help children feel that they are receiving personal attention from the adults at their school.

On the bulletin board outside of her office, Mrs. Jones will display a collage that shows every kind of family. Families representing different combinations of familial composition will be invited to the classrooms. Nishimura (1995) notes that "It is equally important for monoracial children to be exposed to diverse family configurations so that they begin to see differences as being normal" (p. 55). Multicultural and diversity projects will be ongoing throughout the school year so that the celebration of a particular ethnic group is not limited to one day, week, or month. The developmental multicultural program has been put together by a teacher committee and Mrs. Jones and approved by the administration and school board.

As a member of the School Advisory Committee, Mrs. Jones is working with the committee to revise registration forms that request the racial identity of children. School personnel are aware of the need for this revision, as other interracial families are moving into the school district. Adding the category of "mixed race," "multiracial," or "interracial" will help mixed-race children realize that all parts of their racial heritage are important.

Counseling With Multiracial Children

Adler (1987) states: "The most important goal in counseling biracial students is to increase awareness of their heritage and to enhance the dignity and respect given to that heritage" (p. 58). Building a cross-cultural relationship with the multiracial child may be challenging for the counselor, especially if this is the first time the child has seen a counselor or if the child is not a self-referral. Because there was an elementary counselor at Joe's former school and Mrs. Jones had already visited his classroom, establishing a relationship with Joe was not a challenge.

Mrs. Jones will draw on her training in cross-cultural counseling to work with Joe. She is aware of the misuse of cultural knowledge with clients and that counselors "walk a tightrope" when using cultural information in cross-cultural counseling (Wehrly, 1995, 1996). If we have no information on the cultures of our clients, we may make blunders in counseling that can destroy the cross-cultural working relationship. If we use the cultural information that we have to stereotype our clients, we deny their uniqueness as individuals and may insult or demean them (Kleinman, 1985). These cautions apply also to cross-cultural work with children. An insensitive assumption that might be made in work with a Black-White child such as Joe would be to tell him that you expect that the family enjoys eating "chitlins and collards" rather than asking Joe about his food preferences.

It is assumed that the counselor will consider the cognitive developmental level of the child in selection of counseling techniques and interventions. If the child has any physical limitations, the counselor may also need to consider these in working with that child. Joe is a bright fourth grader and has no physical limitations, so Mrs. Jones will be able to use a variety of counseling techniques with him.

Because Joe was referred to the counselor by his teacher, an age-appropriate discussion of the referral was included in the first session. Mrs. Jones explained the teacher's referral in positive terms, stating that

Joe's teacher thought he might profit from talking with a counselor. Then she asked Joe to tell her how he felt about being referred to a counselor. Joe stated that he felt somewhat nervous but knew that the counselor was there to help.

There are special issues to consider in working with interracial children, but the counselor must remember that the problem with which the interracial child needs help may be unrelated to her or his interracial status (Wardle & Baptiste, 1988). Racial identity issues are not usually the expressed reason for referring that child to a counselor (McRoy & Freeman, 1986; Nishimura, 1995). Instead, mixed-race children have more often been referred for problems of academic achievement, inattentiveness in the classroom, social isolation, negative attitudes toward adults, or aggressive behavior toward peers.

Joe's referral to the counselor *is* related to his interracial status and the aggressive behavior Joe displayed when he felt insulted by a peer. Joe's teacher also expressed concern over Joe's withdrawn behavior in the classroom. Joe has already expressed regret for fighting in response to being insulted. Mrs. Jones may encourage more exploration of Joe's feelings about that incident if he wishes to discuss it. It will be important to determine how Joe has responded in the past when he has been asked the question, "What are you, anyway?" This discussion can lead into an exploration of Joe's personal feelings about his racial identity and whether he has talked with his parents about this. Alternative responses to questions on racial identity can be explored and role played during counseling sessions.

One of the most valuable tools that any counselor has in working with children is the ability to listen actively. In the busy world in which today's children live, it may be rare for them to have an adult listen actively for even a few minutes. Through culturally sensitive active listening, the counselor can gain a perspective on how mixed-race children view their worlds and how they feel about the situations in which they live. Because Joe is new to the community and still misses his old friends, he is especially appreciative of the opportunity to talk freely with an understanding person like Mrs. Jones.

The use of feeling reflections and open-ended questions is often conducive to helping children talk more freely about their problems. Strong feelings about children's interracial identity need to be heard and validated. Brandell (1988) states that some interracial children who have rejected the racial heritage of one of their parents may display massive feelings of guilt as well as feelings of disloyalty. The feelings of ambivalence described by Jacobs (1977, 1992) are common. Joe has already moved through the stage where he felt ambivalent about his dual racial heritage and sequentially showed preference for his White mother and then for his Black father. He no longer shows perceptual distortion in identifying the skin coloring of other members of the family. Joe does remember feeling guilty about rejecting his White mother during the stage when he identified only with his Black father. He and Mrs. Jones have discussed whether this guilt still bothers him.

Interracial children like Joe may be the targets of racist behaviors. At times the counselor's role will be to help children sort out the reality of racist behaviors in other people. The counselor and Joe have discussed when and how to stand up to people who direct racist behaviors toward him. Joe let Mrs. Jones know that when his peers call him racist names in the future, he will let them know he thinks they are trying to hurt him. He is also willing to tell his peers and adults that he is mixed Black and White because his father is Black and his mother is White. Role playing and role reversal were valuable in teaching Joe when and how to use these responses. Concurrent classroom discussions on racism and antiracist behavior are occurring to help all children understand their role in reducing racism in the school environment.

The counselor may need to sort out the reticence of some children to talk about problems and determine if there is a cultural component that has conditioned these children to show respect through silence or not share family secrets with anyone outside of the family. A cultural impact on nonverbal communication and on the use of space may also be evident. Joe does not seem reluctant to talk about his problems, so Mrs. Jones does not see a need to explore cultural influences on talking about personal problems.

Joe tells Mrs. Jones that his family rarely talks about race or racial issues. He thinks it is because his mother and father are so busy with their demanding occupations. Joe says that his grandparents are "neat people" and show lots of love for him. He rarely gets to see his grandparents, however, because they live hundreds of miles away. Joe knows that Mrs. Jones will be meeting with his parents. He has given her permission to tell them he would like to have more family discussions on race and how to handle racist behaviors.

In individual counseling with interracial children, Mrs. Jones finds play media helpful with those who are reticent to talk. Some girls and boys enjoy working with clay; others express themselves well through art activities. Crayons and paints in shades of different skin, hair, and eye colors should be available if the counselor is going to have children use art media. If the counselor uses family figures, it will be very important for the child to have access to family figures in various skin colors and with features representing all different groups of people of color. Joe loves to draw pictures and is enjoying drawing while he talks with Mrs. Jones.

School counselors rarely have time to engage in in-depth or extended therapy with children. When children manifest problems that need more time or expertise than the counselor can give, they are referred to a mental health center where counselors have appropriate backgrounds for the evaluation and follow-up treatment of mixed-race children.

Many of the problems manifested by interracial children brought for therapy are related to the racial identity confusion felt by the interracial child, even though the verbalized presenting problem(s) may not indicate this (Brandell, 1988). This seems to be particularly true with interracial children whose parents are divorced or separated and who rarely, or never, see the absent parent or any of the absent parent's extended family. Often the interracial child has been raised almost solely with people of the racial heritage of the parent with whom the child lives. In cases like this, it is especially important for the counselor to take time to listen to the child and the adult who has brought the child for therapy. Assessing how interracial children view their racial identity will be important. Working with both the child and significant adults in the child's life may be necessary in implementing both assessment and treatment.

Brandell (1988) describes psychoanalytic self-psychology therapy with a biracial Black-White child referred mainly because of escalating behavior problems at school and hostile and defiant behavior at home. According to Brandell (1988), the child was suffering from ongoing empathic failures of her parents, especially "traumatic disappointments in her father" (p. 185). The child's father had left a live-in relationship with her mother before the child was born. He was erratic in keeping promises to spend time with the child. Brandell gives a detailed account of the techniques and processes that he used in therapy with this biracial child. The most effective techniques were reciprocal drawing and storytelling games. The use of the self-psychological perspective helped the therapist identify problems in self-identity development of the interracial child.

Counselor Work With Parents and Families of Multiracial Children

As Wardle (1990) notes, parents in interracial families are raising their children in a variety of ways: as "just children" with no attention given to their racial identity, as children with one racial identity (sometimes that of the parent of color), or as children with a rich interracial status. Children of interracial heritage have genes from both parents and from the racial heritages of both parents. The genes from one parent do not dominate the genes from the other parent.

As noted in Chapter 3, identity development, including racial identity development, begins in early childhood and continues throughout the individual's life. The child's physical appearance will have an important role in the child's racial identity development. For many interracial children, skin color differences may be one of the first differences they notice about themselves and others. Parents play an important role in how well the mixed-race child is able to accept her or his physical appearance.

Counselors and teachers working with mixed-race children should meet with parents to discuss issues that are unique to the interracial family. Mrs. Jones has asked Joe's parents to meet with her. Because both of them are busy during the day, Mrs. Jones will meet with them during the evening sessions scheduled for parent conferences with teachers. After talking with them about their perspectives on Joe, Mrs. Jones plans to use some of Wardle's (1990) questions in her conference with Joe's parents:

1. How do the people in your home identify your mixed-race children?
2. How is Joe's interracial status supported and nurtured in the home?
3. What do you, as Joe's parents, want the school staff to do to support your choice for Joe's interracial identity?
4. How do you respond to negative comments directed at your sons by others? How are you teaching Joe to respond to these negative comments?
5. What do the people in your home do to "positively reaffirm your children's differences [to Joe]" (Wardle, 1990, p. 25)?

Parents can be encouraged to offer age-appropriate answers to questions their interracial children ask. Emphasis on positive aspects of the child's mixed-race heritage is important (Lyles, Yancey, Grace, & Carter, 1985). This information should be given in a straightforward manner as soon as children become racially aware and raise concerns about their racial heritages.

Counselors can help validate and support a family lifestyle that celebrates the interracial family heritage (Adler, 1987). Parents can be encouraged to help their children develop an awareness of the racial and ethnic cultures of both mother and father. Because Joe's grandparents live some distance away, his parents can be encouraged to participate with Joe in cultural activities to acquaint him with both sides of his racial heritage.

As noted earlier, Joe has asked Mrs. Jones to let his parents know that he would like them to take time to talk about race in family discussions. She will do this and encourage them to discuss ways they might implement these discussions. Mrs. Jones is prepared to respond to questions that Joe's parents may have on this issue. She will show empathy for their long working hours and the resulting difficulty in finding time for family discussions, but she will also stress the importance of these opportunities for family communication.

As discussed in Chapter 3, Jacobs (1977, 1992) describes two kinds of information that parents can present to their children to help the children's biracial identity development. First, parents can help their children to see that they are part of both parents and part of the race of each of these parents. Children can be taught that they are part _____ and part _____. In addition, biracial parents can teach their children that they (the children) are different from the race of either parent. Parents can help their children decide on a biracial or interracial identity, such as "I'm mixed," "I'm biracial," "I'm interracial," or "I'm multiracial." Use of the questions suggested by Wardle should help Mrs. Jones determine what Joe's parents have done, or are doing, to address these issues with their son.

Parents may need assistance in understanding and working with the racial ambivalence that biracial children normally show between the ages of about 4½ and 8 years. It may help parents to know that "The working through of ambivalence seems primarily influenced by parents' supportive interest in the child's racial feelings and secondarily by a racially supportive environment outside of the family" (Jacobs, 1992, p. 205). This underscores the importance of a biracial or multiracial environment for the interracial child. Mrs. Jones may want to find out how Joe's parents help their sons through this difficult stage.

Counselors sometimes educate the interracial family through making them aware of support groups, recommending appropriate books to use with their interracial children, and helping families develop approaches for addressing myths related to interracial individuals and families. Joe's parents share with Mrs. Jones that they participated in an active interracial support group in the area in which they previously lived. They intend to continue with this group even though it is now a greater distance to drive to meetings. Mrs. Jones may explore the possibility of Joe's parents helping to get a new interracial support group started in the community where they now live.

Counselor Roles in Work With a
Transracially Adopted College Student

As suggested in previous chapters, children of ethnic minority or international backgrounds who are adopted into European American families may at times experience scrutiny from peers because of their physical features and appearance. Additional concerns related to adjustment and identity development may be observed among children who are adopted at an older age and by parents who do not avail themselves of or make available to the child experiences geared toward easing the adjustment process and enhancing the child's positive development (Okun, 1996; Wardle, 1992b).

Case Example

Nathan Hobbs is a 20-year-old college student who was born in the Dominican Republic. At the age of 5 years, Nathan was adopted by a White family from affluent Wilton, Connecticut. The community in which he was raised is an all-White New England community, and Nathan attended schools with all White students. His contact with people of color was virtually nonexistent.

Although it was no secret to Nathan that he was adopted, his parents always treated him as though he were their natural-born child. Nathan, however, has always known that he was different. He has dark skin and curly hair, features that his peers have always pointed out and even ridiculed. Throughout school, Nathan's White peers called him names and made negative comments about his appearance. During high school, it was difficult for him to get dates with White female students. Once, when he queried a female friend about her decision not to date him, he was informed that it was because he was "too dark" and that people would not approve.

In an effort not to bring attention to his differences, and as a result of not having availed themselves of supportive connections and resources when Nathan was young, Nathan's adoptive parents have done nothing to address issues of culture, ethnicity, and race. Nathan has grown up in a European American environment and world and has had no exposure to his Latino-Dominican culture and heritage. When he has attempted to talk with his parents about his negative experiences with his peers, his parents have explained his peers' behavior away as "playing."

Nathan is a first-semester college sophomore now. The university he attends has a diverse student population, including a large international student population. Nathan is a biogenetics major, like his father was. He does extremely well academically and plans to go on for a Ph.D. He has also considered medical school. The students that Nathan has felt most comfortable with have been White, although he periodically experiences uncomfortable moments around them. This happens when they make remarks and jokes about students of color and references to his dark skin. He has also had some uncomfortable moments with White professors who have made assumptions about his upbringing as a result of his physical appearance.

One of his professors commented that Nathan had probably consumed a lot of rice and beans growing up. Nathan has not eaten rice and beans and does not recall doing so even as a small child.

Out of curiosity and a desire to be more socially active, Nathan has attempted to engage and participate in campus events sponsored by groups set up for students of color. This has been awkward for him. He has observed that he differs from these students in terms of behaviors and attitudes. Nathan began having severe stomach pains and headaches toward the end of the previous spring semester. At about that time he met a Puerto Rican American woman named Martha. The two had been in math class together, had been attracted to each other, and had begun to spend a lot of time together. Martha, as it turns out, is from the Bronx, New York, where she lives with her parents and three brothers.

Nathan's White roommate and some of his White male friends made sexually perverted comments about Nathan and his relationship with Martha. Martha is friends with many of the students of color. Nathan has observed that some of Martha's friends are not particularly fond of or trusting of the White people (staff or students) on campus because of perceptions of having been ill-treated. Additionally, some of them have referred to Nathan as the "White boy" because of knowledge of his associations with predominantly White students. A month before the end of the spring semester, Martha invited Nathan to go home to New York with her. Nathan found this experience to be very different from what he was used to. Martha's neighborhood and community were very diverse. In fact, Nathan recalls that he and his White peers growing up would never have gone into the area alone. Martha's family is Catholic and (culturally) Puerto Rican, with the language, food, and customs he had read about in a magazine. Nathan enjoyed himself but felt awkward at times because of the obvious differences in their upbringing and home life. He also felt that Martha's family found him peculiar because, although he looked Latino, he had a different last name and he appeared uncomfortable with their Latino customs and ways.

With summer drawing near, Martha and Nathan had begun to discuss where the relationship was going and what their intentions were for maintaining the relationship. They both decided that they wanted to continue the relationship and would make plans to talk by phone and probably see each other, too. Up to this point, Nathan had only shared with Martha that he lived in Connecticut in a predominantly White community and that he was an only child. Nathan had spoken with his parents by phone numerous times since the start of his relationship with Martha, but he put off telling them about her. He was concerned whether his parents would accept her Latino background and whether she would be accepting of his White parents. As Nathan became more involved in the relationship, he began having more stomach discomfort and headaches. The relationship continued during the summer, with Nathan putting off giving his parents any details about Martha. In addition, Nathan did a lot to cover up the significance of his relationship with his parents in his dealings with Martha. In essence, he lived a dual life during the summer, learning more about Latino heritage through his encounters with Martha, her family, and her friends, while at the same time continuing to maintain his connections with his all-White community in Wilton.

Nathan's stomachaches and headaches persisted through the summer and were worse at some times than at others. As they continued to intensify, Nathan and his parents became concerned to the point of scheduling an appointment with the family physician. Numerous medical tests were conducted; however, the final reports from these tests suggest that there was no medical origin for his physiological symptoms. The physician attributed the problems to stress and anxiety and recommended that Nathan seek counseling on returning to school.

Intervention

During the initial consultation and intake session at the university counseling center, Nathan provided the above background information. He explained that his doctor had suggested that he come to the center for help because he was having stomach problems and headaches, which were possibly due to stress and anxiety. He talked about his relationships with Martha and with his parents and shared that it was becoming more and more difficult for him to keep his lives separate.

Dr. Ritter, the staff person at the university counseling center who is working with Nathan, is taking a developmental approach in addressing Nathan's presenting concerns. His work with Nathan began with an assessment and exploration of where Nathan is developmentally. Taking this approach has provided some useful information relative to Nathan's identity development, his emancipation from his family, and his social skills. This information has also been useful in determining the root of his stress and anxiety, which have been manifested through physiological symptoms. Nathan agrees that he feels socially awkward, particularly around students of color. He also agrees that on many levels it has been difficult to separate from his parents and the upbringing they provided. He further indicates that his major in school has even been somewhat influenced by his parents. In looking at Nathan from the perspective of Marcia's Identity Development Model (1980), Nathan is in the identity foreclosed status for some aspects of his identity development; for others, he is either in the identity diffused status or the identity moratorium status. As a result of his upbringing and the fact that only in the recent year has he begun to consider himself as a Latino-Dominican individual, it is very clear that Nathan is in the identity moratorium status with regard to his ethnic and cultural identity. Dr. Ritter interprets his observations to Nathan, including his speculation that his headaches and stomachaches are the result of stress and anxiety that he is experiencing because of the concerns they have been discussing. This makes sense to Nathan, especially as he realizes that the symptoms began around the time that he and Martha began to see each other.

Dr. Ritter has given Nathan some suggestions on options and alternatives for dealing with the feelings of stress and anxiety. Many of these options center around relaxation techniques and exercise, two things that Nathan acknowledges he has not done much of. They also discuss the option of journaling. This option is a good one for Nathan because he enjoys writing and is able to express his feelings more when he writes. Nathan agrees to bring his journal to sessions so that he can discuss some of its content with Dr. Ritter. As Dr. Ritter continues his work with Nathan, he focuses on assisting Nathan in exploring his identity. As much of his presenting story centered around issues related to his ethnic and cultural identity, Dr. Ritter pays particular attention to this aspect of Nathan's identity development.

Dr. Ritter and Nathan explore and discuss what it means for Nathan to acknowledge his Latino-Dominican heritage now. Nathan acknowledges some sadness regarding those aspects of his heritage that he has lost. He also acknowledges some confusion and frustration toward his parents for the lack of significance they placed on his maintaining his heritage. He reveals that he feels guilty about being upset with them, particularly because they have been so good to him. He also indicates feeling guilty about what now feels like a rejection of them and the background he was raised in. On the other hand, Nathan is eager to learn more about and to become more comfortable with his heritage. For this purpose, Dr. Ritter feels bibliotherapy would be useful, and he recommends some appropriate reading material, which includes *Adoption: The Facts, Feelings, and Issues of a Double Heritage* (Duprau, 1989); *Families Are Different* (Pellegrini, 1991); and *Being Adopted* (Rosenberg, 1984). In addition, Dr. Ritter suggests that another way for Nathan to become more familiar with his heritage is to seek out activities, programs, and groups that give him more exposure to his ethnic and cultural roots. Dr. Ritter also suggests that Nathan augment their work together by joining a support group for transracially adopted individuals.

With the help of individual therapy provided by Dr. Ritter and the support group, Nathan is able to come to terms with his feelings of guilt and frustration toward his parents. Through both venues, Nathan is empowered to discuss with his parents his feelings of conflict regarding his relationship with Martha. Upon attending some support group meetings for parents of transracially adopted children at Nathan's request, his parents begin to understand how their previous view of things was not beneficial for Nathan's growth and development as a Latino male. Regarding Nathan's relationship, they express interest in meeting Martha and her family when Nathan is ready for this to occur.

Nathan acknowledges to Dr. Ritter that he has been concerned about sharing his parent's background with Martha. He fears that she will be angry with him for hiding her from them and vice versa. He further fears that she will feel that he has been ashamed of her all of this time. Further exploration reveals that on some levels Nathan has been fearful of telling Martha about his parents out of fear for how she might react toward them and toward the fact that they are wealthy European Americans. He also acknowledges that he has felt somewhat ashamed of her and her background, mostly because since the age of 5 years he has felt ashamed of his background and has wanted to be White. His relationship with Martha has placed him in contact with aspects of himself that he had lost and had even come to deny. This has been a struggle for him. Nathan and Dr. Ritter continue their discussions about Nathan's identity, his relationship with his parents, and his relationship with Martha. With the help of his individual sessions and his support group meetings, he is able to come up with a strategy for telling Martha the truth about his background and his parents. He is empowered to do so after having a discussion with a fellow support group member who had experienced the same thing.

In working with Nathan, it was very important for the counselor to discuss and explore Nathan's feelings regarding his "double life," as he referred to it. In helping Nathan to explore these feelings, the counselor was able to assist Nathan in identifying feelings of stress and anxiety that were manifested by the headaches and stomachaches. The two then explored the underlying origins of Nathan's stress and anxiety. In discussion, it was discovered that Nathan was experiencing feelings of guilt and confusion related to concerns that he was betraying his parents by attempting to discover his true roots and heritage. He felt guilty keeping Martha from his parents because it suggested that she was not "good enough" and that he was ashamed of who she was. In further discussion, Nathan acknowledged that he was a little ashamed of Martha and her Latino background. It frightened him to discover that he was also in some ways ashamed of himself because of his own Latino background. The teasing and jeering Nathan had received from his White peers for "being dark," and the bigoted attitudes of White students toward people of color, had contributed to Nathan's feelings of shame. In addition, the lack of importance that was given to Nathan's true ethnicity and culture by his parents contributed to Nathan's perception of Latino heritage as insignificant.

Nathan's parents would have done well to have consulted with a counselor or educator trained in these issues on how to go about assisting Nathan in dealing with the onslaught of comments about his features and skin color. These experiences are, unfortunately, quite common for children with distinctly different features from their White adoptive families. Families who adopt transracially often benefit from opportunities to discuss their feelings and concerns about raising a child of a different race and culture and with different physical features. These discussions can provide them with tools and other helpful information about how to deal with questions and comments they encounter, as well as helping the child deal with difficult situations he or she may encounter with peers and other adults. A child may also benefit from opportunities to discuss feelings about the obvious differences (Okun, 1996). Support groups for multiracial families can provide a wide range of support and information for families both prior to and after the adoption has taken place.

It is obvious that much of Nathan's struggle centers around issues related to his identity development as a Latino-Dominican individual. As he was adopted at the age of 5 years, Nathan's early childhood had been spent in his native environment. Although adolescence has special significance with regard to ethnic and racial identity development, younger children are often aware of some ethnic and cultural differences (Markstrom-Adams & Spencer, 1994; Spencer & Dornbusch, 1990). Nathan's connection to everything associated with his Dominican identity was stripped away on his adoption. An important thing to have been considered at the time of the adoption was how Nathan (in light of his age) was dealing with the separation from his home and cultural environment. In addition, a useful way to help smooth the transition for Nathan would have been for the family to have availed themselves of resources providing assistance to families that adopt internationally. As Wardle (1992b) suggests, White parents who adopt transracially should expose their children to a variety of people and should adjust their lifestyle to meet the needs of the children. Such exposure might have provided information to Nathan's parents that could have assisted them in helping Nathan accept and assimilate into his new environment more easily while at the same time continuing to build on his awareness and acceptance of his identity as a Dominican.

According to Santrock (1997), as children grow into adolescence, their ability to interpret ethnic and cultural information, reflect on the past, and speculate about the future increases. Cognitive maturity in adolescence results in teenagers of ethnic or minority backgrounds becoming intensely aware of the evaluations and perceptions the White majority holds towards persons of color (Comer, 1988). Hence, in Nathan's case, resources that would have enhanced awareness of his cultural background and assisted him in developing a positive perspective of his ethnic heritage and roots would have been helpful. These might also have helped him to develop social and relationship skills and strategies for dealing more effectively with the ridicule, teasing, and rejection that he received throughout school.

Reading materials that appear to be useful for adults who are considering adoption or have adopted include *Raising Adopted Children: A Manual for Adoptive Parents* (Melina, 1987); *The Adoption Resource Book* (Gilman, 1992); and *Are Those Kids Yours? American Families With Children Adopted From Other Countries* (Register, 1990).

Counselor Roles in Work With Multiracial Adults[2]

Root (1994) and Logan, Freeman, and McRoy (1987) recognize that mixed-race people rarely come to counseling asking for help in resolving overt issues related to their interracial heritages. Instead, they may be referred for social work services for problems such as "inadequate social relationships, parent-child conflicts in their current families, and inadequate separation from their families of origin" (Logan et al., 1987, p. 14). To be effective in working with these problems, helping service workers usually have to address racial identity issues also.

A case example of a hypothetical mixed-race client, Carol, is presented. Following this, concepts and interventions from the work of Root (1990, 1994, 1997a, 1997b, 1998), Logan et al. (1987), Spickard (1989), other authors, and the clinical observations of the authors of this book will be presented as these concepts relate to counselor work with Carol.

Case Example

Carol is a 35-year-old White-Japanese female who has come for counseling because of issues related to lack of acceptance by coworkers, loneliness, and feeling that she does not belong. Carol has worked as a receptionist and bookkeeper at a local insurance office since she finished a 2-year secretarial program at a local, rural, Midwest community college. She is the youngest of three children of a White U.S. serviceman who met and married her

Japanese mother while he was with the Army of Occupation in Japan after World War II.

In 1952, Carol's mother came to the United States from Japan with her father and two older bothers. Her mother did everything she could to become "American" and to please her husband and in-laws when she arrived in a rural Midwest community as the Japanese wife of a recently discharged White serviceman. She learned to communicate in English, to cook "American" dishes, and to sew "American"-style clothing. She joined the local Lutheran church of which her husband and family were members.

Carol's two brothers are in their late 40s and have lived on the West Coast since they finished graduate degrees in chemistry and mathematics. Both brothers married White American women and have maintained minimal contact with their parents and Carol since they married. Because Carol's brothers were in college when she was born, she never felt close to them.

Carol's paternal grandparents have always praised her for being such a good "American" granddaughter. They take great pride in the fact that she looks more like her blonde Scandinavian father than her Japanese mother. Since she was a little girl, Carol's paternal grandparents have praised her for keeping her hair short and permed.

Carol says that she never felt close to either set of her grandparents. Before their deaths in the 1980s, her Japanese grandparents occasionally wrote to her mother. Because the letters were written in Japanese, Carol had to depend on her mother to translate them. To Carol, the letters seemed overly formal and lacking in real news.

Carol remembers that in high school she was encouraged to run for queen of the junior-senior prom because she was told that she had that "exotic" look. She also remembers being teased behind her back for her "Chinka, Chinka Chinaman" eyes.

As she was an outstanding student in both high school and community college, Carol's classmates came to her for help with their homework. Often, they talked Carol into letting them copy her homework. Carol noticed, however, that the same students did not ask her to join their social cliques. Being the only biracial student in her school led to the feeling that she did not belong in any group. Her energies were spent toward serving as editor of the high school newspaper and high school yearbook.

For years, Carol has attended and worked in the church of her father's family. Recently she realized that she receives little satisfaction through her church-related activities.

Carol is also dissatisfied with the relationships that she has had with men. She notices that men seem to be attracted to her "exotic" appearance but do not want to enter into deep and long-lasting relationships. She feels that she has been exploited sexually. Lately, she has turned down all opportunities for male companionship.

At work, Carol has suffered verbal sexual harassment from her boss, but she feels that she cannot complain because he pays her well and gives her generous fringe benefits. Her coworkers are polite and friendly on a superficial basis, but she never seems to develop real friendships with them.

Carol asks the counselor what to do about living life as an outsider most of the time. She says that at times she is very lonely and depressed and stays in her apartment reading or watching television when she has free time.

Implications for Counselor Interventions From the Work of Maria Root (1990, 1994, 1997a, 1997b, 1998)

Six general themes related to being interracial are discussed by Root (1994): uniqueness, acceptance and belonging, physical appearance, sexuality, self-esteem, and identity. Suggestions for applying these themes in working with Carol follow.

Uniqueness. Root emphasizes the importance of being different and unique to the multiracial person and states that this theme interfaces with all of the other themes. Uniqueness can be assessed as pathological if not understood by counselors.

Some multiracial adults personalize events that seem to perpetuate their feeling of being misunderstood and different. This lifestyle can lead to a style of communicating that provides much context to help others understand one's uniqueness, a style of communicating that may look compulsive and even paranoid to others. Carol gives very detailed and contextualized accounts when she discusses her problems.

Living as a unique individual all of one's life sometimes leads to strong feelings of isolation and depression. Carol gives evidence of this. Her ongoing feelings of depression will need to be addressed by the counselor.

Some multiracial adults take on the role of being the chief negotiator between their family, their peers, and the larger society because they feel they have a better understanding of the situation than others do. Carol took on this role as she got older. Her behavior might be interpreted as indicative of a dysfunctional family, when in reality it is the larger society in which the multiracial individual lives that is dysfunctional. The counselor may want to explore with Carol whether she wishes to continue in this negotiator role.

Acceptance and Belonging. Mixed-race individuals' challenges to feeling accepted start as soon as they are old enough to interact with their worlds, and these challenges have been described throughout this book. A lifetime of hearing insensitive questions and comments does not provide a basis for feeling that one belongs. Feelings of rejection, anger, and hurt need to be validated by the counselor.

Difficulties in belonging are intensified during adolescence when peer group acceptance and inclusion are paramount. Social and environmental barriers to acceptance and belonging have continued into adulthood for Carol. The counselor needs to let Carol know that she hears this from Carol. Some issues to explore related to gaining acceptance may be those of feeling exploited in both the past and the present, denouncing part of her racial heritage, and moving to a feeling that it is OK to be and feel different.

Physical Appearance. Root (1994) notes three types of unique experiences related to physical appearance that the mixed-race person might encounter. One is having a name that does not fit with one's appearance. This can lead to questions as to whether this is a married name or whether one is adopted. The counselor could ask Carol if having a name that does not fit her "exotic" appearance has ever bothered her.

The endless stares that the interrracial individual encounters are the second type of experience and can lead to feelings of ongoing evaluation by others. Carol has not reported this, but it may be an area for exploration. Root cautions against the therapist's assuming that these feelings are irrational because there may be a strong reality base present for this interpretation. Cognitive therapy to dispel irrational beliefs may not be appropriate.

The third experience suggested by Root relates to the flexibility of appearance of which the multiracial individual is capable. This heightens the need for the person to establish a consistent internal identity that does not need to be validated by the environment. Root notes that the behavior of "playing with" one's flexible look beyond adolescence "does not necessarily indicate pathology or lack of a stable identity, but may instead reflect valuing of different pieces of the person's identity . . . or even a conscious or unconscious challenge to society's social order" (Root, 1994, p. 468). In Carol's case, the counselor may need more information before deciding how much Carol needs validation from her environment to feel good about her physical appearance. Also, how do situational contexts influence the way Carol's physical appearance is perceived, and how does she respond? The counselor might encourage Carol to "play with" racial and ethnic appearances at times to see how others respond.

Sexuality. The area of sexuality is an appropriate one for counselors to explore with multiracial clients, but sexuality as an issue for multiracial men has rarely been addressed in the counseling literature. The old myths of the exotic sexual attraction of the multiracial female persist. For some women, the myth provides permission to be sexual; for others, the myths seem to lead to curtailment of sexuality.

Carol recognizes that her sexual relationships were affected by both racial and gender stereotypes and a desire to feel accepted. She admits both sexual and emotional abuse by some of the males with which she had relationships. Her boss's harassment has been limited to inappropriate verbalization and innuendo. Counselor and client work in the area of sexuality is needed and will probably overlap with the areas of acceptance, belonging, and physical appearance.

Self-Esteem. For some multiracial people, the concept of being different or special equates with the necessity to be outstanding or extra good to feel positive about themselves. When mixed-race individuals base their worth on this necessity to excel, they may develop fragile feelings of self-worth and fluid concepts of self. The person with a fluid concept of self will be very controlled by external events. When an individual has a fluid concept of self, "the self is as the self does" (Wehrly, 1995, p. 16).

The historic perceptions of interracial individuals as having a higher incidence of problems and poor self-esteem seem to have become self-fulfilling prophecies for some multiracial people. However, recent studies of nonclinical biracial adolescents and adults (Alipuria, 1990; Cauce et al., 1992; Field, 1992, 1996; Gibbs & Hines, 1992; Grove, 1991; Hall, 1980, 1992, 1997; Kerwin, 1991; Tizard & Phoenix, 1995) have not supported the negative self-esteem perceptions of earlier writers.

An area for the counselor to explore with Carol is how much her feelings of self-worth are based on external evaluations. Root cautions that counselors who are not aware of their own internalized oppressive beliefs about multiracial people may inaccurately conclude that low self-esteem is the basis of the problems of multiracial clients.

Identity. Identity issues of multiracial individuals have been addressed throughout this book. Having a sense of identity equates with having a sense of belonging.

The models of multiracial identity development delineated in Chapter 3 provide the counselor with a framework for assessing levels of development and choices of identity made by the interracial client. Selection of an appropriate model (or models) to use in client assessment and treatment will depend on counselor-client interactions and on the client's style of learning.

Root's (1990) metamodel for four possible resolutions of biracial identity provide a framework for exploration with Carol. In how many of these four possible resolutions for her biracial identity has Carol operated in the past and present? How does she describe her comfort level in the various resolutions?

Root's most recent Ecological Identity Model (1998), introduced and discussed in Chapter 3, provides a wide framework of issues for assessment and exploration in counseling sessions with Carol. Root's model includes many aspects of racial identity to be considered within a lifespan focus. Inherited influences that are influential in identity development are languages at home, parent's identity, nativity, extended family, names, home values, sexual orientation, and phenotype. Traits influencing identity are temperament, social skills, talents, and coping skills. Social interactions with community that influence identity include those experienced at home, at school or work, in the community, with friends, and outside the community. Influencing all three major categories is the regional history of race relations. The interaction of all of these variables makes up the individual's racial or ethnic identity. Gender is an influence that is depicted as surrounding all of these variables.

Because Root's (1998) ecological identity model was developed for multiracial Asian Americans, this model should be particularly appropriate for counselor use with Carol. A bright person like Carol might be interested in reading this chapter by Root and discussing it with her counselor.

Application of Concepts from Logan, Freeman, and McRoy's (1987) Ecological Approach

This approach is composed of assessment and interventions and is discussed separately under these categories. In actual practice, the interventions overlap and are interrelated rather than being a neat two-phase process.

Several possible components of assessment are suggested. One is direct observation of the client. Listen for the way in which Carol refers to her racial identity and whether others are blamed for racial identity issues. Watch for nonverbal behaviors that indicate uneasiness and discomfort when racial identity issues are discussed.

Three other process-oriented procedures are recommended for assessment in work with biracial clients. The first is the use of the *genogram*. Work on the genogram can begin as soon as a positive working relationship is established with Carol. Construction of the genogram will help the counselor and Carol examine racial identity issues in the context of the family.

Logan et al. (1987) suggest that in addition to the usual areas explored with the genogram (relationships within the family, patterns of communication, emotional cut-offs, family events that have been significant, assignment of roles, etc.), additional questions need to be explored with interracial clients.

Areas unique to Carol's interracial family that should be explored are racial heritages of parents and siblings; attitudes of family members toward the different racial heritages of family members; how the family and others assign racial labels to Carol; how Carol labels herself racially; patterns and themes in both functional and dysfunctional areas across generations (this might be impossible to assess for the relatives still living in Japan); moves that the family has made related to their mixed-race heritage; and "lifestyle factors related to racial backgrounds such as childbearing practices, health patterns, dietary habits, causes of stress and patterns of coping with it, occupational choices, marital relationships, and economic conditions" (Logan et al., 1987, p. 15). Gathering this information can also help the counselor and Carol summarize both strengths and problems and provide a basis for discussion of changes that she desires.

The second process-oriented technique recommended by Logan et al. (1987) is the construction of an ecomap. This can be adapted to reflect issues unique to being of mixed race. The same kinds of connecting lines and symbols to indicate relationships are used in the ecomap as in a genogram. In a sense, the ecomap (see Figure 6.1) is an extension of the genogram. Members of the client's family or household are listed in a large central circle. Other important people and social systems are represented outside the central circle. Connections between those in the central circle and people and social systems outside are indicated using connecting lines like those used in a genogram to represent relationships.

Construction of the ecomap with Carol can follow discussion of her genogram. The ecomap provides the opportunity to observe what external social systems (such as work, education, extended family, peers, and leisure time) are placing pressures on Carol. Carol's ecomap will probably indicate current stressful situations at work and a past stressful situation with a live-in boyfriend. Relations with her paternal grandparents indicate a tenuous situation in spite of much energy flowing in both directions. Her past involvement with her church has meant a heavy outflow of energy but a tenuous situation as far as satisfaction derived for Carol. The counselor and Carol should work to find a balance between supportive and conflictual environmental relationships.

Logan et al. (1987) recommend exploring additional questions with interracial clients as the client and counselor work to develop the ecomap:

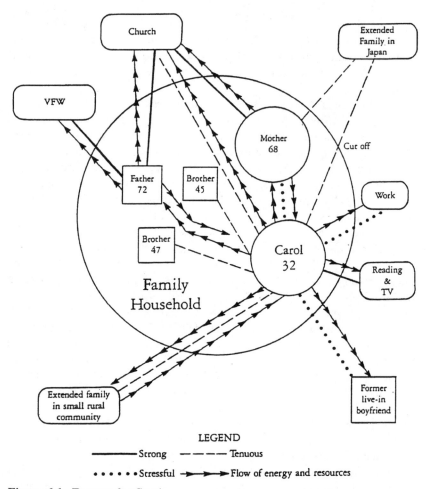

Figure 6.1. Ecomap for Carol

NOTE: Revised and reprinted with permission from the *Journal of Intergroup Relations* (the official quarterly of the National Association of Human Rights Workers), 1987, *15*(1), 20.

1. What role models for positive racial identity development are present? In Carol's case, her brothers may be the only role models she can name.

2. What cut-offs related to racial identity issues are there? Carol is totally cut off from her maternal relatives and somewhat cut off from her brothers.

3. When and how did these cut-offs occur, and how have these cut-offs affected the client's functioning? The cut-off with Carol's maternal grandparents began before she was born and was finalized when they died. The partial cut-offs with her brothers occurred when she was a young girl. This has left her feeling isolated from her brothers.

Table 6.1 The Cultural Continuum

Denial of the Importance of Race and Culture (Color-Blind Perception)	*Complete Assimilation Within the Dominant Culture*	*Complete Assimilation Within the Relevant Minority Culture*	*Bicultural or Multicultural*
Advantages			
Avoidance of pain associated with working through racial identity issues	Greater acceptance by and blending in with dominant culture when successfully assimilated	Greater group support, maintenance of the minority culture, and possibility of positive racial identity	Increased ability to function effectively in two or more cultures, access to resources in the dominant culture as well as those of minority culture, and cultural maintenance
Disadvantages			
Lack of connection with and support from any culture, denial of self, and failure to handle conflictual views of society about racial identity	Loss of culture, traditions, and group support from the rejected cultural group	Limited access to resources available in dominant culture and loss of opportunities to learn about the positive effects of cultural diversity	Risk of failing in two or more cultures and emotional stress associated with adapting to more than one culture

NOTE: Reprinted with permission from the *Journal of Intergroup Relations* (the official quarterly of the National Association of Human Rights Workers), 1987, *15*(1), 17.

4. Can Carol's negative perspectives of her situation be reframed to reflect positive strengths? If Carol becomes interested in studying her Japanese heritage, she may find positive Japanese values that are reflected in her daily life. She might also find it advantageous to play with her identity in various situations and see what results this brings.

5. Are there sources of support for Carol that she has ignored? Carol's brothers and their families might provide support if she can learn how to reach out to them.

The third process-oriented intervention strategy recommended by Logan et al. (1987) is the *cultural continuum* (see Table 6.1). "The cultural continuum is a tool for helping mixed-race clients identify how they have adapted to their racial background and the potential consequences for that stance and other options" (Logan et al., 1987, p. 16). It shows the extent of individual adaptation to one's racial background. On the cultural continuum, this adaptation to racial background ranges from denying the importance of culture associated with one's racial background to biculturalism. The cultural continuum notes both advantages and disadvantages for the four different cultural identifications along the continuum.

Carol can study the continuum with the counselor, decide where she "is" on the scale, and discuss issues such as the following with the counselor:

1. What behavioral evidence supports Carol's selection of a particular spot on the continuum?

2. How aware is Carol of the various options for identification with her cultural heritages and of the advantages and disadvantages of these levels of cultural identifications?

3. Is Carol satisfied with her current choice of cultural identification? If not, what does she want to do about making changes in identification with her cultures of origin?

4. Are there individuals on Carol's genogram or ecomap that represent the cultural continuum point where she would like to be? How might Carol use the identified individual (or individuals) to aid in moving to a different spot on the cultural continuum? This discussion might lead to an interest by Carol in meeting other people of mixed-race heritage through joining an interracial support group. If there is none in her immediate area, the counselor might help her search for such a support group in an urban area to which Carol could commute.

Use of these three process-oriented techniques during the counseling session (the genogram, the ecomap, and the cultural continuum) is a non-pathological procedure to help interracial clients clarify "if and to what extent racial identity issues are problematic for them" (Logan et al., 1987, p. 16). The procedures also help in identifying positive supports for Carol's racial identity.

Other Counseling Techniques

Because Carol is an avid reader, she might enjoy searching the literature to study both sides of her racial heritage, the Swedish American and the Japanese, as out-of-session assignments. There are a host of sources for studying culture and history. One of the traditional sources is the *Harvard Encyclopedia of American Ethnic Groups,* edited by Thernstrom (1980). Two of the nine volumes of the more recent *Encyclopedia of World Cultures* could provide more comprehensive information on Carol's Swedish and Japanese background: Volume 4, *Europe,* edited by Bennett (1992), and Volume 5, *East and Southeast Asia,* edited by Hockings (1993). Parts I and II, "Japanese Americans" and "Madam Butterfly Revisited," of Spickard's (1989) book *Mixed Blood,* contain information on the history and background of the Japanese in America. Part II, "Madam Butterfly Revisited," might be of special interest to Carol because it delineates the sociopolitical situation in Japan when her father served with the U.S. Army of Occupation and met and married her mother. Part II also discusses the sociopolitical situation in the United States at the time that her parents came to settle here. The content of Part II could provide material for discussions with her parents.

Novels are a meaningful way for some people to learn about culture and history. In recent decades, many ethnic novels and autobiographies have made the best-seller lists (e.g., *I Know Why the Caged Bird Sings,* Angelou, 1970; *The Joy Luck Club,* Tan, 1989; *Bless Me Ultima,* Anaya, 1973; *Snow Falling on Cedars,* Guterson, 1995; and *Soul Catcher,* Herbert, 1984). Novels and stories about biracial and interracial people are of more recent origin (e.g., *Black, White, Other: Biracial Americans Talk About Race and Ethnicity,* Funderburg, 1994; *The Color of Water: A Black Man's Tribute to His White Mother,* McBride, 1996; *Divided to the Vein: A Journey into Race and Family,* Minerbrook, 1996; *Life on the Color Line,* Williams, 1995; and *The Sweeter the Juice,* Haizlip, 1994). Carol might find it interesting to read how these people have, and are, negotiating life in the United States. Content of any of this kind of out-of-session reading could make for interesting discussions with the counselor.

Counselor Roles in Work With a Multiracial Couple

As cited in Chapter 2 of this book, the issues, concerns, and challenges faced by contemporary multiracial couples are very similar to those faced by all couples in today's society. This is not to say, however that multiracial couples do not at times have concerns that may be related to differences in the ethnic and cultural worldviews of each partner. Couples can be helped to effectively deal with challenges and concerns in such a way that it is not suggested that there is something pathologically wrong with them as a couple because they are ethnically or culturally different. Instead, they can be taught to deal with their issues and concerns in a manner that allows them to affirm and celebrate each other's cultural heritage (Ibrahim & Schroeder, 1990).

Case Example

Xiu is a 33-year-old native-born Chinese woman who immigrated to the United States after college. She is married to 36-year-old Chris, an Irish-Scottish American. Xiu and Chris have been married for 11 years. They have a son, Tan, who is 6 years old, and a daughter, Reisa, who is 4 years old. Xiu is a trained interpreter. She worked part-time when the children were younger but currently works full-time for an international corporation. Chris is a bonds consultant for a major corporation.

Recently, the two have been having communication difficulties and disagreements related mainly to parenting issues and roles. Xiu, raised in China with her three brothers who are now all in major professional positions, has very strong feelings about her son's education. Each night, whether he has homework or not, Xiu insists that Tan spend at least an hour doing school work. This carries over into the weekends as well. Chris believes that this is too much for a six year old. His parents, who live across the street from the couple and are always around, also express concern that this is too much. Xiu often hears comments about allowing Tan to play and watch television. Xiu remembers her parents reinforcing the need for her brothers to do their homework. She is concerned that Tan may not grow to be a successful man if he slacks off on his education now.

Xiu respects her in-laws and appreciates the help they provide; however, at times she feels misunderstood and ganged up on by Chris and his parents because of her parenting style and views. Chris and his parents have also complained about Xiu's response to the children when they are ill. Xiu has had training and is very knowledgeable about the use of Chinese herbs and medicine for the treatment of illness. She frowns on some American medical traditions, and (ironically, her husband feels) many of her methods for treating the children when they are sick have been successful. Chris refers to this as Chinese voodoo. Xiu becomes insulted.

Chris's view of Asian women, prior to meeting Xiu, was that they were submissive and doting. Xiu is very loving and caring of her family, but Chris feels that she does not necessarily put the family and their home first in the way he expected she would. Because of her dedication to her work, she does not always have the time to be at home to clean, prepare meals, do laundry, and so on. To Chris and his parents' surprise, Xiu expects that Chris will help with these things. Chris's mother was always around to do these things for his family. Even once Chris became older and moved out on his own, he was close enough to his parents to be able to rely on his mother for help. She would often do his laundry and give him care packages of cooked food for the week to take back to his apartment when he was still a bachelor. These issues have caused many difficulties for the couple, and, feeling over-whelmed, they have decided to seek counseling.

Intervention

Dr. Santoro listens to the presenting concerns of Xiu and Chris with great empathy. As she observes and listens to the dynamics and issues in the relationship, she begins to ponder questions about the cultural identity, backgrounds, and worldviews of both partners. Her work with Xiu and Chris begins with an examination and assessment of the cultural backgrounds and worldviews of both. According to Ibrahim and Schroeder (1990), helping partners to clarify and understand each person's worldview and cultural background can provide them with useful information for understanding the values that they each bring into the relationship. In addition, such exploration is useful for assisting the couple in better understanding the source and context of their conflicts. A typical approach to counseling would entail assisting the couple in making changes in individual behavior that is seen as maladaptive to the relationship, but such change in this case is likely to be more counterproductive than not. Thus a key part of the therapeutic work and process with Xiu and Chris involves helping them to understand and accept each other's cultural background and worldview in a manner that allows for compromise in the relationship.

Prior to the discussion of their cultural background and worldviews with Dr. Santoro, neither Xiu nor Chris had ever discussed these matters when alone with each other. Chris had no idea about the significance that the education of men in the family held in Xiu's culture and in her own family of origin. In addition, he had just assumed that her role was that of being subservient to him and to their family. Likewise, Xiu did not understand the significance that Chris's being free to work hard outside the home and be the primary provider had for him and for the men in his family. She now at least had an understanding of where his resistance to do more work when he arrived home was coming from.

Ibrahim and Schroeder (1990) suggest the use of questions adapted from McGoldrick, Giordano, and Pearce (1982) in continuing to work with couples after the cultural background and worldview assessment has been conducted. The questions include:

1. How does each partner define the relational problem?
2. What does each partner perceive as a solution to the problem? How have the partners attempted to resolve things previously?

3. To whom would each partner generally turn for help?

4. Considering their cultural backgrounds and families of origin, what are typical patterns regarding communication rules, expression of intimacy, boundaries, and so on for each of them?

5. How does each partner's culture affect his or her perception of roles and expectations in the relationship?

6. How are life cycle stage and transitions defined and dealt with by the cultural groups to which each partner belongs?

7. How did each partner's cultural group respond to immigration? What is the generation of each partner?

8. What are the spiritual and religious backgrounds of each person and how do these views affect his or her view of the relationship?

9. What are some pros and cons of having a counselor of the same or different background in this particular situation?

Responding to these questions gives Xiu and Chris a better understanding of how their individual backgrounds have contributed to their views and interactions in the context of their relationship. Having this understanding, they feel less defensive and no longer have the view that each is out to get the other or that their attitudes and behaviors are about attacking the other personally. They begin to see each other in a different light.

In addition to considering Xiu and Chris's responses to the above questions and as suggested by Ibrahim and Schroeder (1990), further exploration includes a discussion with both partners regarding the following: their satisfaction with the relationship overall, the effectiveness of communication between them, the stability and level of commitment to the relationship, and their individual expectations regarding family roles. Xiu and Chris realize that they are very commited to their relationship and to their family. They realize too that their lack of awareness and understanding of the impact of culture and worldview on their individual lives and personas influenced how they communicated with each other in the past. They also see how all this has affected their expectations and perceptions of each other's roles and responsibilities.

Continuing to follow the recommendation of Ibrahim and Schroeder (1990), Dr. Santoro begins to introduce the psychoeducational aspect of work with cross-cultural couples. They begin this part of the process by reexamining all three of their worldviews. Dr. Santoro's worldview has been important to consider throughout this process for its possible connection to and influence on his view of this couple and the problems it is presenting. In discussion of each partner's worldview, it is important for the counselor to help the couple see the similarites and differences that exist between the partners. In so doing, the counselor can also help them focus on the strengths and weaknesses of their relationship. Here, the impacts of gender, cultural and religious factors, life stage and age factors, career issues, and so on are important to consider. Dr. Santoro has helped Xiu and Chris to see that although there are differences between them, there are also similarities, which served to attract them to each other and have also helped to cement their relationship. The differences he has pointed out are not necessarily negative either, as they have helped in providing some variance in the relationship. The two seem willing to discuss openly the impact of gender, cultural and religious factors, life stage, careers, and so on, as they have already acknowledged an awareness and understanding of the role these things have played with regard to their concerns.

Both Xiu and Chris seem quite eager to participate in the exercises Dr. Santoro introduces, which require each of them to take on the other's cultural worldviews, beliefs, roles, and so on. These exercises provide them with real insight into those cultural and personal factors that have influenced who they both are as individuals, and they are able to empathize more with each other's position and stance. The knowledge component of the process recommended by Ibrahim and Schroeder (1990) is an opportunity for the partners to gain additional information regarding each other's culture through bibliotherapy. Dr. Santoro recommends some books and also gives the couple reading materials that he has acquired over the years. It is suggested that by reading this additional information, the partners will become more equipped with an understanding of where each other is coming from. In the next five to 10 sessions, Dr. Santoro spends time teaching Xiu and Chris culturally appropriate attitudes and skills that allow them to relate better to each other and thus have their individual emotional, functional, and relationship needs met. Time is spent assisting Xiu and Chris in learning to empathize with each other in times of crisis, which entails listening to each other in a manner that suggests to the other that the listener understands what has been said. Once Dr. Santoro feels that they have mastered this phase of the process, he encourages them to verbalize their individual feelings in a culturally appropriate way.

Finally, Dr. Santoro leads Xiu and Chris in what Ibrahim and Schroeder (1990) have referred to as culture-specific problem solving and conflict resolution. This entails assisting both partners in establishing a mutually acceptable agreement that takes into consideration the cultures of each. With the purpose of the skill component being that of reinforcing the awareness, affective, and knowledge components of the process, the partners are helped to understand that their conflicts can be resolved if they are willing to make a commitment to acknowledging and accepting each other's cultural identities and to learning culturally appropriate communication and conflict resolution skills. Xiu and Chris are committed to their relationship and thus agree to be more cognizant of cultural factors when working through their conflicts. In addition, the focus on cultural identity and worldview in the therapeutic process has assisted Xiu and Chris in being more aware of the cultural identity development needs of their children. They both appear more open to opportunites that allow for the cultural enrichment of the entire family.

Counselor Roles in Work With a
Gay Multiracial Family

The number of gay and lesbian individuals and couples raising children is showing a dramatic increase. Concerns regarding the psychosocial development and well-being of these children is often called into question as a result of overt or masked homophobia. As the number of gay and lesbian families continues to increase, it becomes imperative that professional counselors be made aware of the challenges these families face, while at the same time learning to work with these families from a strengths model and perspective, thus empowering them in their ability to be resilient (Okun, 1996).

Case Example

Sam, a 10-year-old African American child, was a year old when his mother walked out, never to be seen or heard from again. A young woman with no family of her own to speak of, she had been a relatively unstable person most of her life, and Roger, Sam's father, had basically taken care of her since they met. The two were never married, but Eva had become pregnant with Sam a year after the relationship began. When Sam was 5 years old, Roger met and became involved with a White man by the name of Martin. The three have lived together as a family since Sam was 7 years old. Roger works for an internationally affiliated company and travels periodically. Martin is a social worker. They live in South Hadley, Massachussetts, in a relatively diverse community.

The three spend a lot of time together when they are all at home and have a great relationship. Sam is very close to Martin, who takes care of him (like a parent) when Roger is away on extended international business trips. Six months ago, Roger heard through a distant cousin of Eva's that she had been found dead of a drug overdose. Roger had attempted to answer Sam's periodic questions about his mother as best as he could. To his amazement, Sam did not seem to have an emotional connection to his mother or his memories of her. He was simply curious. After Roger shared the news of Eva's death with Martin, the two decided to tell Sam together. Again, Sam seemed to take the news quite well.

Roger and Martin had been talking for some months prior to the news of Eva's death about where their relationship was going and how Sam fit into the picture. Because of the closeness of their relationship, Martin had expressed interest in adopting Sam. However, the barrier to this was uncertainty as to whether Eva would ever return and attempt to reclaim Sam and file custody for him. Roger and Martin had also talked of having a commitment ceremony to bind their relationship. The news of Eva's death resulted in Roger and Martin addressing the questions of their relationship and Sam's adoption by Martin again. This time, however, their discussions seemed more stressful, as there were many other questions to respond to, including how and when to tell Sam about the nature of their relationship, how Sam would feel about Martin's desire to adopt him, how they would, as a family, deal with being a gay and a multiracial family. The stress of these concerns has resulted in Roger and Martin being short with each other at times. Martin, being a social worker, understands that the stress is related to the fact that they are about to embark on some major decisions related to them as a couple and them as a family. The person that will be most affected by these decisions will be Sam. With this in mind, Martin suggests to Roger that they see a counselor who can help them through this process.

Intervention

Linda has worked with many gay and lesbian couples and families and knows what a challenge dealing with issues related to becoming a family can be. She sees strengths, however, in Roger and Martin's relationship, based on some of the factors surrounding their circumstances, and she points these out. First, although potentially difficult for Sam from a developmental standpoint, the fact that he never really knew Eva and has had a strong bond with Roger and then with Martin is a positive thing. Linda suggests that although attention does need to be given to any remaining questions or emotions Sam may have related to his mother or to not having a mother, the strength of the bond that has existed between Roger, Martin, and Sam needs to be emphasized and cultivated. Additionally, Roger and Sam as a unit have always been supported by Roger's family of origin and by his extended family. The entire family is aware of Roger's sexual orientation, and although they had difficulties accepting this at first, they have all rallied around Roger and Sam and now even accept Martin. Again, Eva had very few relatives of whom she was aware. Roger's only contact with any of Eva's relatives was with a distant cousin whom he met only once. Sam's only knowledge of Eva's relatives is the cousin of whom his dad had spoken. Martin's family has known about his sexual orientation for years and they are accepting of Roger and delighted at the prospect of the two parenting Sam together officially.

The real concern for Roger and Martin is how to be open about their relationship to Sam. Roger and Martin are pretty open about their relationship to neighbors and people in their local community. In addition, the teachers and administrators at Sam's school are aware. Linda knows of several support groups in the area, and she refers Roger and Martin to these so that they can begin to talk with others about coming out to Sam and about how to deal with his feelings around this, particularly related to his peers. She also recommends several books and encourages Roger and Martin to read them and to share their thoughts and feelings about the readings with her as they meet each week and prepare to make this part of their journey. The recommended books include *Gay and Lesbian Parents* (Bozett, 1987); *The Final Closet: The Gay Parents' Guide for Coming Out to Their Children* (Corley, 1990); *The Lesbian and Gay Parenting Handbook* (Martin, 1993); *There's Something I've Been Meaning to Tell You: Lesbian and Gay Parents Come Out to Their Children* (MacPike, 1989).

In helping Roger and Martin to prepare for the process of disclosing their relationship to Sam, Linda also attempted to help them understand what they might expect from Sam. They role played numerous scenarios to aid in this process. As Okun (1996) indicated, children of gay and lesbian parents not only experience different feelings than their parents with regard to sexual orientation, they also experience different feelings than their peers whose parents are heterosexual. A child's experience of "differentness" may result in isolation and withdrawal. Being in a home environment where these issues and concerns are discussed openly can be a source of safety and support for the child. Linda encouraged Roger and Martin to carefully examine their priorities and the long- and short-term possible consequences of their relationship failing, the realities of parenting, and the realities of dealing with homophobia and racism. She also encouraged

them to examine and be clear about how they will manage and provide for Sam's overall positive development. In doing this, she also emphasized the need for them to consider practicalities, including preparation of legal documents, particularly in the event that something would happen to either or both of them. Gay partners caring for children together need to be aware of the legal alternatives available to them and to their families (Martin, 1993).

Once Sam was told about Roger and Martin's relationship and about Martin's desire to adopt him, the three became involved in family sessions. Sam handled the news of their sexual orientation well and was excited about the idea of Martin adopting him officially. As they began the adoption process, Linda felt that it was important to explain and discuss with Sam the varied reactions that he might receive from his peers, both because of Roger and Martin's sexual orientation and perhaps because of the differences in their racial and cultural backgrounds. She suggested that because he might experience a variety of feelings about all of this new information and the possible changes in his life, he might want to read some books both with Roger and Martin and on his own. She also suggested that he might want to talk with other children who had two moms or two dads. The books she recommended included *How Would You Feel If Your Dad Was Gay?* (Heron & Maran, 1991); *Jenny Lives With Eric and Martin* (Bosche, 1983); and *Daddy's Roommate* (Willhoite, 1990). Linda emphasized the importance of Sam feeling free to ask any questions or discuss any concerns or feelings he might have with Roger and Martin and during the sessions with her.

Okun (1996) recommended the use of ecograms in assisting gay families in mapping the support resources available to them. In addition to the support they have from their families of origin, extended family, and from the groups they have already become involved with, Linda suggests that Roger, Nathan, and Sam continue to avail themselves of options in the community that allow them to address and celebrate the multiple heritages and cultures that are prevalent in their family as well. According to Okun (1996), an important aspect of a clinician's work with gay and lesbian families is that of providing information on resources and networks available for support and encouraging family members to use these resources. As counselors, we are called upon to advocate for our clients. Okun (1996) suggests that with the gay and lesbian community, this means not only being aware of support resources in the gay and lesbian communities but also advocating for improvement in the quality of services being provided to this population by the community at large.

Notes

1. Adapted by permission from Wehrly (1996), pp. 55-69). No further reproduction is authorized without written permission from the American Counseling Association.

2. Adapted by permission from Wehrly (1996), pp. 124-139. No further reproduction is authorized without written permission from the American Counseling Association.

References

Abdullah, S. B. (1996). Transracial adoption is not the solution to America's problem of child welfare. *Journal of Black Psychology, 22,* 254-261.

An act to execute certain treaty stipulation relating to Chinese, 1882, 8 U.S.C.A. @185 261 (West 1970).

An act to amend an act entitled: An act to execute certain treaty stipulation relating to Chinese, 1884, 8 U.S.C.A. @185 262-298 (West 1970).

An act to conserve and develop Indian land and resources, 1934, 25 U.S.C.A. @185 461-476 (West 1970).

Adams, C. L., & Kimmel, D. C. (1997). Exploring the lives of older African American gay men. In B. Greene (Ed.), *Ethnic and cultural diversity among lesbians and gay men* (pp. 132-151). Thousand Oaks, CA: Sage.

Adams, J. L. (1997). *Multiracial identity development: Developmental correlates and themes among multiracial adults.* Unpublished doctoral dissertation, Ohio State University, Columbus.

Adejando-Wright, M. N. (1985). The child's conception of racial clarification. In M. B. Spencer, G. K. Brookings, & W. R. Allen (Eds.), *Beginnings: The social and affective development of Black children* (pp. 185-200). Hillsdale, NJ: Lawrence Erlbaum.

Adler, A. (1987). Children and biracial identity. In A. Thomas & J. Grimes (Eds.), *Children's needs: Psychological perspectives* (pp. 56-61). Washington, DC: National Association of School Psychologists.

Alexander, R., & Curtis, C. M. (1996). A review of empirical research involving the transracial adoption of African American children. *Journal of Black Psychology, 22,* 223-235.

Alien Land Laws of 1913, 1 Stat. Calif. Amend. Codes Chap. 113 (1913).

Alipuria, L. L. (1990). *Self esteem and self label in multiethnic students from two Southern California state universities.* Unpublished master's thesis, California State University, Los Angeles.

Allman, K. M. (1996). (Un)natural boundaries—mixed race, gender, and sexuality. In M.P.P. Root (Ed.), *The multiracial experience: Racial borders as the new frontier* (pp. 277-290). Thousand Oaks, CA: Sage.

Alstein, H., Coster, M., First-Hartling, L., Ford, C., Glasoe, B., Hairston, S., Kasoff, J., & Grier, A. W. (1994). Clinical observations of adult intercountry adoptees and their adoptive parents. *Child Welfare, 73,* 261-269.

Anaya, R. (1973). *Bless me Ultima.* Berkeley, CA: Quinto Sol.

Anderson, K. S. (1993). Ethnic identity in biracial Asian Americans. *Dissertation Abstracts International, 54*(09-B), 4905.

Anderson, R. A. (1981). *Government and business* (4th ed.). Cincinnati, OH: Southwestern.

Angelou, M. (1970). *I know why the caged bird sings.* New York: Random House.

Aronson, D. (1995). Heroic possibilities. *Teaching Tolerance, 4*(1), 11-15.

Arredondo, P., & Glauner, T. (1992). *Personal dimensions of identity model.* Boston: Empowerment Workshops.

Arredondo, P., Toporek, R., Brown, S., Jones, J., Locke, D. C., Sanchez, J., & Stadler, H. (1996, January). *Operationalization of the multicultural counseling competencies.* Alexandria, VA: Association for Multicultural Counseling and Development.

Attneave, C. (1982). American Indians and Alaska native families: Emigrants in their own homeland. In M. Goldrich, J. K. Pearce, & J. Giordano (Eds.), *Ethnicity and family therapy* (1st ed., pp. 55-83). New York: Guilford.

Aubrey, R. (1995, February 19). A White boy who learned he was Black crossed color line anyway. *San Diego Union-Tribune,* p. A-35.

Azoulay, K. G. (1997). *Black, Jewish, and interracial: It's not the color of your skin, but the race of your kin and other myths of identity.* Durham, NC: Duke University Press.

Bagley, C. (1993). *International and transracial adoptions: A mental health perspective.* Brookfield, MA: Avebury.

Bailey, T. A. (1975). *The American pageant: A history of the republic* (5th ed.). Lexington, MA: D. C. Heath.

Bartholet, E. (1993). *Family bonds—Adoption and the politics of parenting.* New York: Houghton Mifflin.

Bates, J. D. (1993). *Gift children: A story of race, family, and adoption in a divided America.* New York: Ticknor & Fields.

Beech, H. (1996, April 8). Don't you dare list them as "other." *U.S. News & World Report,* 56.

Bennett, L. A. (Ed.). (1992). *Encyclopedia of world cultures: Europe* (Vol. 4). Boston: G. K. Hall.

Blau, M. (1998, December/January). Multiracial families. *Child, 12*(10), 96, 98, 103.

Borders, L. D. (1993a, September/October). Going it alone: The challenge of single parenting. Adoption decisions. *Ours,* 28.

Borders, L. D. (1993b, August 8). Let's give single mothers the benefit of the doubt. *Greensboro News & Record,* p. F3.

Borders, L. D. (1995a, January/February). Where's daddy? *Adoptive Families,* 46-48.

Borders, L. D. (July/August, 1995b). The passing of innocence. *Adoptive Families,* pp. 26-28.

Bosche, S. (1983). *Jenny lives with Eric and Martin.* London: Guernsey.

Bowles, D. D. (1993). Bi-racial identity: Children born to African-American and White couples. *Clinical Social Work Journal, 21,* 417-428.

Bozett, F. W. (1987). *Gay and lesbian parents.* New York: Praeger.

Finkel, D. (1997, May 4). Now say goodbye to Diane. *Washington Post Magazine,* pp. 7, 9-17.

Fischer, A. (1994, January/February). "Is she adopted?"—Multicultural families find haven in UU churches. *The World,* pp. 24-27.

Folaron, G., & Hess, P. M. (1993). Placement considerations for children of mixed African American and Caucasian parentage. *Child Welfare, 72,* 113-125.

Frankenberg, R. (1995). *White women, race matters: The social construction of Whiteness.* Minneapolis: University of Minnesota Press.

Funderburg, L. (1994). *Black, White, other: Biracial Americans talk about race and ethnicity.* New York: William Morrow.

Galens, J., Sheets, A., & Young, R. (Eds.). (1995). *Gale encyclopedia of multicultural America* (Vol. 2). Detroit, MI: Gale Research.

Gay, K. (1987). *The rainbow effect: Interracial families.* New York: Franklin Watts.

General Allotment Act of 1887, 25 U.S.C.A. § 331 (West 1983).

Gibbs, J. T. (1985). Treatment relationships with Black clients: Interpersonal vs. instrumental strategies. In C. B. Germain, P. Caroff, P. L. Ewalt, P. Glasser, & R. Vaughn (Eds.), *Advances in clinical social work practice* (pp. 184-195). Silver Spring, MD: National Association of Social Workers.

Gibbs, J. T. (1987). Identity and marginality: Issues in the treatment of biracial adolescents. *American Journal of Orthopsychiatry, 57,* 265-278.

Gibbs, J. T. (1989). Biracial adolescents. In J. T. Gibbs, L. N. Huang, & Associates (Eds.), *Children of color: Psychological interventions with minority youth* (pp. 322-350). San Francisco: Jossey Bass.

Gibbs, J. T., & Hines, A. M. (1992). Negotiating ethnic identity: Issues for Black-White biracial adolescents. In M.P.P. Root (Ed.), *Racially mixed people in America* (pp. 223-238). Newbury Park, CA: Sage.

Gibbs, J. T., & Moskowitz-Sweet, G. (1991). Clinical and cultural issues in the treatment of biracial and bicultural adolescents. *Families in Society: The Journal of Contemporary Human Services, 72,* 579-591.

Gilman, L. (1992). *The adoption resource book* (3rd ed.). New York: Harper Perennial.

Goddard, L. L. (1996). Transracial adoption: Unanswered theoretical and conceptual issues. *Journal of Black Psychology, 22,* 273-281.

Goetz, B., Barstow, S., Farrell, P., & Palya, N. (1998, January). Federal law will speed adoption process. *Counseling Today, 40,* 1, 10, 12.

Gopaul-McNicol, S. (1996). Critique of "A review of the research on transracial adoption," *Journal of Black Pscyhology, 22,* 270-272.

Graham, S. (1996). The real world. In M.P.P. Root (Ed.), *The multiracial experience: Racial borders as the new frontier* (pp. 37-48). Newbury Park, CA: Sage.

Greene, B. (1994a). Ethnic-minority lesbians and gay men: Mental health and treatment issues. *Journal of Consulting and Clinical Psychology, 62*(2), 243-251.

Greene, B. (1994b). Lesbian women of color: Triple jeopardy. In L. Comas-Diaz & B. Greene (Eds.), *Women of color: Integrating ethnic and gender identities in psychotherapy* (pp. 389-427). New York: Guilford.

Greene, B. (1997). Ethnic minority lesbians and gay men: Mental health and treatment issues. In B. Greene (Ed.), *Ethnic and cultural diversity among lesbians and gay men* (pp. 216-239). Thousand Oaks, CA: Sage.

Greene, B., & Boyd-Franklin, N. (1996). African American lesbian couples: Ethnocultural considerations in psychotherapy. *Women and Therapy, 19*(3), 49-60.

Griffith, E.E.H., & Silverman, I. L. (1995). Transracial adoptions and the continuing debate on the racial identity of families. In H. W. Harris, H. C. Blue, & E.E.H. Griffith (Eds.), *Racial and ethnic identity: Psychological development and creative expression* (pp. 95-114). New York: Routledge.

Grosz, G. (1989). From sea to shining sea. . . . A current listing of interracial organizations and support groups across the nation. *Interrace, 1,* 24-28.

Grosz, G. (1997, Fall). Just the facts. *Interrace, 8*(1), 6.

Grove, K. J. (1991). Identity development in interracial, Asian/White late adolescents: Must it be so problematic? *Journal of Youth and Adolescence, 20,* 617-628.

Gup, T. (1997, April 21). Who is a whiz kid? *Newsweek,* 21.

Gura, M. (1994). The human mosaic project. *Educational Leadership, 51*(8), 40-41.

Guterson, D. (1995). *Snow falling on cedars.* New York: Vintage.

Gutierrez, F. J., & Dworkin, S. H. (1992). Gay, lesbian, and African American: Managing the integration of identities. In S. H. Dworkin & F. J. Gutierrez (Eds.), *Counseling gay men and lesbians: Journey to the end of the rainbow* (pp. 141-156). Alexandria, VA: American Association for Counseling and Development.

Haizlip, S. T. (1994). *The sweeter the juice.* New York: Simon & Schuster.

Hall, C.C.I. (1980). The ethnic identity of racially mixed people: A study of Black-Japanese. *Dissertation Abstracts International, 41*(4-B), 1565-1566.

Hall, C.C.I. (1992). Please choose one: Ethnic identity choices for biracial individuals. In M.P.P. Root (Ed.), *Racially mixed people in America* (pp. 250-264). Newbury Park, CA: Sage.

Hall, C.C.I. (1997). Best of both worlds: Body image and satisfaction of a sample of Black-Japanese biracial individuals. *Amerasia Journal, 23*(1), 87-97.

Harrington, W. (1992). *Crossings: A White man's journey into Black America.* New York: Harper Collins.

Harrison, A. O. (1996). Comments on transracial adoption. *Journal of Black Psychology, 22,* 236-239.

Hayes, S. A. (1996). Cross-cultural learning in elementary guidance activites. *Elementay School Guidance and Counseling, 30,* 264-274.

Hays, P. (1996a). Addressing the complexities of culture and gender in counseling. *Journal of Counseling and Development, 74,* 332-338.

Hays, P. (1996b). Cultural considerations in couples therapy. *Women and Therapy, 19*(3), 13-23.

Hedgeman, R. L. (1987). *Internal and external stressors on interracial marriages: Implications for counseling psychology.* Unpublished doctoral dissertation, University of Nebraska, Lincoln.

Helbig, A. K., & Perkins, A. R. (1994). *This land is our land: A guide to multicultural literature for children and young adults.* Westport, CT: Greenwood.

Helms, J. E. (1990). *Black and white racial identity: Theory, research, and practice.* New York: Greenwood.

Henderson, P. (1990). Black and White protagonists in contemporary fiction: Findings and recommendations for interventions on race relations. *Journal of Multicultural Counseling and Development, 18,* 180-193.

Herbert, F. (1984). *Soul catcher.* New York: Avenel.

Heron, A., & Maran, M. (1991). *How would you feel if your dad was gay?* Boston: Alyson.

Herring, R. D. (1992). Biracial children: An increasing concern for elementary and middle school counselors. *Elementary School Guidance and Counseling, 27,* 123-130.

Herring, R. D. (1995). Developing biracial ethnic identity: A review of the increasing dilemma. *Journal of Multicultural Counseling and Development, 23,* 29-38.

Herring, R. D. (1997). *Multicultural counseling in schools: A synergetic approach.* Alexandria, VA: American Counseling Association.

Herring, R. D. (1999). Experiencing a lack of money and appropriate skin color. *Journal of Counseling and Development, 77*, 25-27.

Hockings, P. (Ed.). (1993). *Encyclopedia of world cultures: East and Southeast Asia* (Vol. 5). Boston: G. K. Hall.

Hollingsworth, L. D. (1997). Effect of transracial/transethnic adoption on children's racial and ethnic identity and self-esteem: A meta-analytic review. *Marriage & Family Review, 25*, 99-130.

Hollingsworth, L. D. (1998). Promoting same-race adoption for children of color. *Social Work, 43*, 104-116.

Hollis, Y. W. (1991, November/December). A legacy of Loving. *New People, 2*, 9-12.

Horning, K. T. (1993). The contributions of alternative press publishers to multicultural literature for children. *Library Trends, 41*, 524-540.

Houston, H. R. (1997). "Between two cultures": A testimony. *Amerasia Journal, 23*(1), 149-154.

Ibrahim, F. A. (1998, March). *Counseling multiracial adolescents.* Paper presented at the Professional Development Institute at the Annual Conference of the American Counseling Association, Indianapolis, IN.

Ibrahim, F. A., & Schroeder, D. G. (1990). Cross-cultural couples counseling: A developmental, psychoeducational intervention. *Journal of Comparative Family Studies, 21*, 193-205.

Indian Arts and Crafts Act of 1990, 18 U.S.C. § 305a-e (Lawyers Cooperative 1995).

In re Estate of Fred Paquet, deceased, 101 Ore. Rep. 393 (Bancroft-Whitney 1922).

Jacobs, J. H. (1977). Black/White interracial families: Marital process and identity development in young children. *Dissertation Abstracts International, 38*(10-B), 5023.

Jacobs, J. H. (1992). Identity development in biracial children. In M.P.P. Root (Ed.), *Racially mixed people in America* (pp. 190-206). Newbury Park, CA: Sage.

Jaimes, M. A. (1995). Some kind of Indian. In N. Zack (Ed.), *American mixed race: The culture of microdiversity* (pp. 133-153). Lanham, MD: Rowman & Littlefield.

Johnson, K. A. (1991). Objective news and other myths: The poisoning of young Black minds. *Journal of Negro Education, 60*(3), 328-341.

Johnson, D. J. (1992). Developmental pathways: Toward an ecological theoretical formulation of race identity in Black-White biracial children. In M.P.P. Root (Ed.), *Racially mixed people in America* (pp. 37-49). Newbury Park, CA: Sage.

Johnson, P. R., Shireman, J. F., & Watson, K. W. (1987). Transracial adoption and the development of Black identity at age eight. *Child Welfare, 66*, 45-55.

Johnson, R. C., & Nagoshi, C. T. (1986). The adjustment of offspring of within-group and interracial/intercultural marriages: A comparison of personality factor scores. *Journal of Marriage and the Family, 48*, 279-284.

Johnson, T. W., & Keren, M. S. (1996). Creating and maintaining boundaries in male couples. In J. Laird & R. Green (Eds.), *Lesbians and gays in couples and families* (pp. 231-250). San Francisco: Jossey-Bass.

Jones, J. S. (1992). *A counseling group for adolescents from interracial families.* Unpublished educational specialist's thesis, James Madison University, Harrisonburg, VA.

Kaeser, G., & Gillespie, P. (1997). *Of many colors.* Amherst: University of Massachusetts Press.

Kahn, D. A. (1993). Transcultural family counseling: Theories and techniques. In J. McFadden (Ed.), *Transcultural counseling: Bilateral and international perspectives* (pp. 109-131). Alexandria, VA: American Counseling Association.

Kalish, S. (1995). Multiracial births increase as U.S. ponders racial definitions. *Population Today: News, Numbers, and Analysis, 23*(4), 1-2.

Kallgren, C. A., & Caudill, P. J. (1993). Current transracial adoption practices: Racial dissonance or racial awareness. *Psychological Reports, 72*, 551-558.

Kandel, B. (1997). *Trevor's story: Growing up biracial.* Minneapolis, MN: Lerner.

Kayleng, A. (1998). The last good nisei man. *Interrace, 8*(3), 10.

Kenney, K. R., & Cohen, J. (1998, May). *Values and communication patterns among Black-White interracial couples.* Paper presented at the Annual Meeting of the Association for the Development of the Person-Centered Approach, Boston, MA.

Kenney, K. R., Kenney, M. E., & Cohen, J. (1994, April). *Interracial marriage, a '90's perspective: Implications for counselors.* Paper presented at the Annual Convention of the American Counseling Association, Minneapolis, MN.

Kerwin, C. (1991). Racial identity development in biracial children of Black/White racial heritage. *Dissertation Abstracts International, 52/07-A,* 2469.

Kerwin, C., & Ponterotto, J. G. (1995). Biracial identity development: Theory and research. In J. G. Ponterotto, J. M. Casas, L. A. Suzuki, & C. M. Alexander (Eds.), *Handbook of multicultural counseling* (pp. 199-217). Newbury Park, CA: Sage.

Kerwin, C., Ponterotto, J. G., Jackson, B. L., & Harris, A. (1993). Racial identity in biracial children: A qualitative investigation. *Journal of Counseling Psychology, 40,* 221-231.

Kezwer, P. (1995). *Worlds of wonder: Resources for multicultural children's literature.* Bothell, WA: Wright Group.

Kich, G. K. (1992). The developmental process of asserting a biracial, bicultural identity. In M.P.P. Root (Ed.), *Racially mixed people in America* (pp. 304-317). Newbury Park, CA: Sage.

Kim, W. J. (1995). International adoption: A case review of Korean children. *Child Psychiatry and Human Development, 25,* 141-154.

Kleinman, A. (1985, February). *Culture in the clinic.* Paper presented at the Third Annual Teachers College Roundtable for Cross-Cultural Counseling, Teachers College, Columbia University, New York City.

Kruse, G. M. (1992). No single season: Multicultural literature for all children. *Wilson Library Bulletin, 66*(6), 30-33, 122.

LaFromboise, T., Coleman, H. L. K., & Gerton, J. (1993). Psychological impact of biculturalism: Evidence and theory. *Psychological Bulletin, 114,* 395-412.

Ladner, J. A. (1977). *Mixed families: Adopting across racial boundaries.* New York: Anchor Press.

Lee, E. (1996). Asian American families: An overview. In M. Goldrich, J. K. Pearce, & J. Giordano (Eds.) *Ethnicity and family therapy* (2nd ed., pp. 227-248). New York: Guilford.

Leland, J. & Beals, G. (1997, May 5). In living colors. *Newsweek,* 58-60.

Levinson, D. (Ed.). (1994). *Encyclopedias of the human experience: Ethnic relations.* Santa Barbara, CA: ABC-CLIO.

Levinson, D. (Ed.). (1995). *Encyclopedia of marriage and the family.* New York: Simon & Schuster/MacMillan.

Lind, M. (1998, August 16). The beige and the black. *New York Times Magazine,* 38-39.

Liu, E. (1998). *The accidental Asian.* New York: Random House.

Lloyd, T. D. (1989). *Perceived ethnic identity, conflicts, and needs of biracial individuals.* Unpublished master's thesis, California State University, Long Beach.

Locke, D. C. (1990). A not so provincial view of multicultural counseling. *Counselor Education and Supervision, 30,* 18-25.

Logan, S. L., Freeman, E. M., & McRoy, R. G. (1987). Racial identity problems of bi-racial clients: Implications for social work practice. *Journal of Intergroup Relations, 15,* 11-24.

Lovett-Tisdale, M., & Purnell, B. A. (1996). It takes an entire village. *Journal of Black Psychology, 22,* 266-269.

Loving et ux. v. Virginia, 18 U.S.S.C.R. Ann. 1010 (1967).

Lydens, L. A. (1988). *A longitudinal study of crosscultural adoption: Identity development among Asian adoptees at adolescence and early adulthood.* Unpublished doctoral dissertation, Northwestern University, Evanston, IL.

Lyles, M. R., Yancey, A., Grace, C., & Carter, J. H. (1985). Racial identity and self-esteem: Problems peculiar to biracial children. *Journal of the American Academy of Child Psychiatry, 24,* 150-153.

Macpherson, D., & Stewart, J. (1992). Racial differences in married female labor force participation behavior: An analysis using interracial marriages. *Review of Black Political Economy, 21,* 59-68.

MacPike, L. (1989). *There's something I've been meaning to tell you: Lesbian and gay parents come out to their children.* Tallahasee, FL: Naiad.

Mamet, D. (1989). *Some freaks.* New York: Viking Penguin.

Marcia, J. E. (1980). Identity in adolescence. In J. Adelson (Ed.), *Handbook of adolescent psychology* (pp. 159-187). New York: Wiley.

Markstom-Adams, C., & Spencer, M. B. (1994). A model for identity intervention with minority adolescents. In S. A. Archer (Ed.), *Intervention for adolescent identity development.* Newbury Park, CA: Sage.

Martin, A. (1993). *The lesbian and gay parenting handbook.* New York: Harper Perennial.

Mays, V. M., & Cochran, S. D. (1988a). The Black Women's Relationship Project: A national survey of Black lesbians. In M. Shepnoff and W. A. Scott (Eds.), *A sourcebook of gay/lesbian health care* (2nd ed., pp. 54-62). Washington, DC: National Lesbian and Gay Health Foundation.

Mays, V. M., & Cochran, S. D. (1988b). Issues in the perception of AIDS risk and reduction by Black and Hispanic/Latina women. *American Psychologist, 43,* 949-957.

Mays, V. M., Cochran, S. D., & Rhue, S. (1993). The impact of perceived discrimination on the intimate relationships of Black lesbians. *Journal of Homosexuality, 25*(4), 1-14.

McBride, J. (1996). *The color of water: A Black man's tribute to his White mother.* New York: Riverhead.

McGoldrick, M., Giordano, J., & Pearce, J. K. (1982). *Ethnicity and family therapy* (1st ed.). New York: Guilford.

McGoldrick, M., Giordano, J., & Pearce, J. K. (1996). *Ethnicity and family therapy* (2nd ed.). New York: Guilford.

McIntyre, D. H. (1994). Gay parents and child custody: A struggle under the legal system. *Mediation Quarterly, 12,* 135-149.

McRoy, R. G., & Freeman, E. (1986). Racial-identity issues among mixed-race children. *Social Work in Education, 8,* 164-175.

McRoy, R. G., & Hall, C.C.I. (1996). Transracial adoptions—In whose best interest? In M.P.P. Root (Ed.), *The multiracial experience: Racial borders as the new frontier* (pp. 63-78). Newbury Park, CA: Sage.

McRoy, R. G., Oglesby, Z., & Grape, H. (1997). Achieving same-race adoptive placements for African American children: Culturally sensitive practice approaches. *Child Welfare, 76,* 85-104.

McRoy, R. G., & Zurcher, L. A. Jr. (1983). *Transracial and inracial adoptees: The adolescent years.* Springfield, IL: Charles C. Thomas.

McRoy, R. G., Zurcher, L. A., Lauderdale, M. L., & Anderson, R. N. (1982). Self-esteem and racial identity in transracial and inracial adoptees. *Social Work, 27,* 522-526.

Melina, L. R. (1987). *Raising adopted children: A manual for adoptive parents.* New York: Harper Perennial.

Melina, L. (1990). Racial identity of children of mixed heritage still controversial. *Adopted Child, 9*(5), 1-4.

Miller, R. L. (1992). The human ecology of multiracial identity. In M.P.P. Root (Ed.), *Racially mixed people in America* (pp. 24-36). Newbury Park, CA: Sage.

Miller-Lachmann, L. (1992). *Our family, our friends, our world: An annotated guide to significant multicultural books for children and teenagers.* New Providence, NJ: R. R. Bowker.

Minerbrook, S. (1996). *Divided to the vein: A journey into race and family.* New York: Harcourt Brace.

Minghan, M. (1996). Census review of ethnic groups raises complex questions. *HR Magazine, 41,* 144.

Morales, E. (1992). Latino gays and Latina lesbians. In S. H. Dworkin & F. J. Gutierrez (Eds.), *Counseling gay men and lesbians: Journey to the end of the rainbow* (pp. 125-139). Alexandria, VA: American Association for Counseling and Development.

Morganthau, T. (1995, February 13). What color is black? *Newsweek,* 62-65.

Murphy-Shigematsu, S.L.H. (1987). The voices of Amerasians: Ethnicity, identity, and empowerment in interracial Japanese Americans. *Dissertation Abstracts International, 48*(4B), 1143.

Nakashima, C. L. (1992). An invisible monster: The creation and denial of mixed-race people in America. In M.P.P. Root (Ed.), *Racially mixed people in America* (pp. 162-178). Newbury Park, CA: Sage.

Nash, G. B. (1982). *Red, black, and white: The people of early America* (2nd ed.). Englewood Cliffs, NJ: Prentice-Hall.

Nash, R. D. (1997). *Coping with interracial dating.* New York: Rosen.

Nishimura, N. J. (1995). Addressing the needs of biracial children: An issue for counselors in a multicultural school environment. *School Counselor, 43,* 52-57.

Nishimura, N. J. (1998). Assessing the issues of multiracial students on college campuses. *Journal of College Counseling, 1*(1), 45-53.

Nishimura, N. J., & Bol, L. (1997). School counselors' perceptions of the counseling needs of biracial children in an urban educational setting. *Research in the Schools, 4*(2), 17-23.

Normandeau, R. (1993). What people are saying about their interracial relations. *Interrace, 4* (5), 21-27.

Okun, B. F. (1996). *Understanding diverse families: What practitioners need to know.* New York: Guilford.

Omizo, M. M., & D'Andrea, M. J. (1995). Multicultural classroom guidance. In C. C. Lee (Ed.), *Counseling for diversity: A guide for school counselors and related professionals* (pp. 143-158). Boston: Allyn and Bacon.

Oriti, B., Bibb, A., & Mahboubi, J. (1996, November). Family-centered practice with racially/ethnically mixed families. *Families in Society: The Journal of Contemporary Human Services, 76*(9), 573-582.

Overmier, K. (1990). Biracial adolescents: Areas of conflict in identity formation. *Journal of Applied Social Sciences, 14,* 157-176.

Page, C. (1996). *Showing my color: Impolite essays on race and identity.* New York: Harper Collins.

Parks, M. R., & Eggert, L. L. (1993). The role of social context in the dynamics of personal relationships. *Advances in Personal Relationships, 2,* 1-34.

Pascoe, P. (1991). Race, gender, and intercultural relations: The case of interracial marriage. *Frontiers: A Journal of Women Studies, 12*(1), 5-18.

Paset, P. S., & Taylor, R. D. (1991). Black and white women's attitudes toward interracial marriage. *Psychological Reports, 69*(3), 753-754.

Patterson, C. J. (1992). Children of lesbian and gay parents. *Child Development, 63,* 1025-1042.

Patterson, C. J. (1997). Children of lesbian and gay parents. *Advances in Clinical Child Psychology, 19,* 235-282.

Pearlman, S. F. (1996). Loving across race and class divides: Relational challenges and the interracial lesbian couple. *Women and Therapy, 19*(3), 25-35.

Pellegrini, N. (1991). *Families are different.* New York: Holiday House.

Penn, M. L., & Coverdale, C. (1996). Transracial adoption: A human rights perspective. *Journal of Black Psychology, 22,* 240-245.

Peplau, L. A., Cochran, S. D., & Mays, V. M. (1997). A national survey of the intimate relationship of African American lesbians and gay men: A look at commitment, satisfaction, sexual behavior, and HIV disease. In B. Greene (Ed.), *Ethnic and cultural diversity among lesbians and gay men* (pp. 11-38). Thousand Oaks, CA: Sage.

Peterson, K. S. (1997a, November 3). For today's teens, race "not an issue anymore." *USA Today,* pp. 1A, 2A.

Peterson, K. S. (1997b, November 3). Interracial dating is no big deal for teens. *USA Today,* p. 10A.

Phinney, J. S. (1989). Stages of ethnic identity development in minority group adolescents. *Journal of Early Adolescence, 9,* 34-49.

Phinney, J. S. (1990). Ethnic identity in adolescence and adulthood: Review of research. *Psychological Bulletin, 108,* 499-514.

Phinney, J. S. (1992). The multigroup ethnic identity measure: A new scale for use with diverse groups. *Journal of Adolescent Research, 7,* 156-176.

Phinney, J. S. (1993). A three-stage model of ethnic identity development in adolescence. In M. E. Bernal & G. P. Knight (Eds), *Ethnic identity: Formation and transmission among Hispanics and other minorities* (pp. 61-79). Albany, NY: SUNY Press.

Phinney, J. S., & Alipuria, L. L. (1990). Ethnic identity in college students from four ethnic groups. *Journal of Adolescence, 13,* 171-183.

Phinney, J. S., & Alipuria, L. L. (1996). At the interface of cultures: Multiethnic/multiracial high school and college students. *Journal of Social Psychology, 136,* 139-158.

Phinney, J. S., & Chavira, V. (1992). Ethnic identity and self-esteem: An exploratory longitudinal study. *Journal of Adolescence, 15,* 271-281.

Phinney, J. S., & Tarver, S. (1988). Ethnic identity search and commitment in Black and White eighth graders. *Journal of Early Adolescence, 8,* 265-277.

Pinderhughes, E. (1995). Biracial identity—Asset or handicap? In H. W. Harris, H. C. Blue, & E.E.H. Griffith (Eds.), *Racial and ethnic identity: Psychological development and creative expression* (pp. 73-93). New York: Routledge.

Plessy v. Ferguson, 41 U.S.S.C.R. 256 (1896).

Ponterotto, J. G. (1991). The nature of prejudice revisited: Implications for counseling intervention. *Journal of Counseling and Development, 70,* 216-224.

Porterfield, E. (1978). *Black and White mixed marriages.* Chicago: Nelson Hall.

Porterfield, E. (1982). Black-American intermarriage in the United States. *Marriage and Family Review, 5,* 17-34.

Poston, W.S.C. (1990). The biracial identity development model: A needed addition. *Journal of Counseling and Development, 69,* 152-155.

Poussaint, A. F. (1984). Study of interracial children presents positive picture. *Interracial Books for Children Bulletin, 15*(6), 9-10.

Protection of Indians and Conservation of Resources Act of 1934, 25 U.S.C.S. § 461 *et seq.* (Bancroft-Whitney 1983).

Ramirez, D. A. (1996). Multiracial identity in a color-conscious world. In M.P.P. Root (Ed.). *The multiracial experience: Racial borders as the new frontier* (pp. 49-62). Newbury Park, CA: Sage.

Ramos, C. (1997). Mommy doesn't look like me! *Interrace, 8*(2), 15-16.

Reddy, M. T. (1994). *Crossing the color line: Race, parenting, and culture.* New Brunswick, NJ: Rutgers University Press.

Register, C. (1990). *"Are those kids yours?" American families with children adopted from other countries.* New York: Free Press.

Roberts, P. O., & Cecil, N. L. (1993). *Developing multicultural awareness through children's literature: A guide for teachers and librarians, grades K-8.* Jefferson, NC: McFarland.

Robinson, T. L., & Howard-Hamilton, M. (1994). An Afrocentric paradigm: Foundations for a healthy self-image and healthy interpersonal relationships. *Journal of Mental Health Counseling, 16*(3), 327-339.

Rodriguez, C. E., Castro, A., Garcia, O., & Torres, A. (1991). Latino racial identity: In the eye of the beholder. *Latino Studies Journal, 2,* 33-48.

Romanc, L. (1997, May). The children left behind. *Good Housekeeping,* 104-107.

Root, M.P.P. (1990). Resolving "other" status: Identity development of biracial individuals. In L. S. Brown & M.P.P. Root (Eds.), *Diversity and complexity in feminist therapy* (pp. 185-205). New York: Haworth.

Root, M.P.P. (Ed.). (1992). *Racially mixed people in America.* Newbury Park, CA: Sage.

Root, M.P.P. (1994). Mixed-race women. In L. Comas-Diaz & B. Greene (Eds.), *Women of color: Integrating ethnic and gender identities in psychotherapy* (pp. 455-478). New York: Guilford.

Root, M.P.P. (1995). The multiracial contribution to the psychological browning of America. In M. Zack (Ed.), *American mixed race: The culture of microdiversity* (pp. 231-236). Lanham, MD: Rowman & Littlefield.

Root, M.P.P. (Ed.). (1996). *The multiracial experience: racial borders as the new frontier.* Thousand Oaks, CA: Sage.

Root, M.P.P. (1997a). Contemporary mixed-heritage Filipino Americans: Fighting colonized identities. In M.P.P. Root (Ed.). *Filipino Americans: Transformation and identity* (pp. 80-94). Thousand Oaks, CA: Sage.

Root, M.P.P. (1997b). Multiracial Asians: Models of ethnic identity. *Amerasia Journal, 23*(1), 29-41.

Root, M.P.P. (1998). Multiracial Americans: Changing the face of Asian America. In L. C. Lee & N. W. Zane (Eds.), *Handbook of Asian American psychology* (pp. 261-287). Thousand Oaks, CA: Sage.

Rosenberg, M. B. (1984). *Being adopted.* New York: Lothrop, Lee & Shepard.

Rosenberg, M. B. (1986). *Living in two worlds.* New York: Lothrop, Lee & Shepard.

Rosenblatt, P. C., Karis, T. A., & Powell, R. D. (1995). *Multiracial couples: Black and White voices.* Newbury Park, CA: Sage.

Saenz, R., Hwang, S-S., Aguirre, B. E., & Anderson, R. N. (1995). Persistence and change in Asian identity among children of intermarried couples. *Sociological Perspectives, 38,* 175-194.

Sandefur, G. D., & McKinnell, T. (1986). American Indian intermarriage. *Social Science Research, 15,* 347-371.

Santrock, J. W. (1997). *Lifespan development* (6th ed.). Boston: McGraw Hill.

Sears, V. L. (1987). *Cross-cultural ethnic relationships.* Unpublished manuscript.

Sebring, D. L. (1985). Considerations in counseling interracial children. *Journal of Non-White Concerns in Personnel and Guidance, 13,* 3-9.

Shireman, J. F., & Johnson, P. R. (1986). A longitudinal study of Black adoptions: Single parent, transracial, and traditional. *Social Work, 31,* 172-176.

Silverman, A. R., & Feigelman, W. (1981). The adjustment of Black children adopted by White families. *Social Casework: The Journal of Contemporary Social Work, 62,* 529-536.

Simon, R. J., & Alstein, H. (1992). *Adoption, race, and identity: From infancy through adolescence.* New York: Praeger.

Simon, R. J., Alstein, H., & Melli, M. S. (1994). *The case for transracial adoption.* Washington, DC: American University Press.

Simpson, G., & Yinger, J. (1985). *Racial and cultural minorities: An analysis of prejudice and discrimination* (5th ed.). New York: William Morrow.

Smith, A. (1997). Cultural diversity and the coming-out process: Implications for clinical practice. In B. Greene (Ed.), *Ethnic and cultural diversity among lesbians and gay men* (pp. 279-300). Thousand Oaks, CA: Sage.

Snipp, C. M. (1997). Some observations about racial boundaries and the experiences of American Indians. *Ethnic and Racial Studies, 20,* 667-689.

Solsberry, P. W. (1994). Interracial couples in the United States of America: Implications for mental health counseling. *Journal of Mental Health Counseling, 4,* 304-377.

Spencer, J. M. (1997). *The new colored people: The mixed-race movement in America.* New York: New York University Press.

Spencer, M. B., & Dornbusch, S. M. (1990). Challenges in studying minority youth. In S. S. Feldman & G. R. Elliott (Eds.), *At the threshold: The developing adolescent.* Cambridge: Harvard University Press.

Spickard, P. R. (1989). *Mixed blood: Intermarriage and ethnic identity in twentieth-century America.* Madison: University of Wisconsin Press.

Spickard, P. R. (1992). The illogic of American racial categories. In M.P.P. Root (Ed.), *Racially mixed people in America* (pp. 12-23). Newbury Park, CA: Sage.

Spickard, P. R. (1997). What must I be? Asian Americans and the question of multiethnic identity. *Amerasia Journal, 23*(1), 43-60.

Steel, M. (1995). New colors: Mixed-race families still find a mixed reception. *Teaching Tolerance, 4*(1), 44-46, 48-49.

Stephan, C. W. (1992). Mixed-heritage individuals: Ethnic identity and trait characteristics. In M.P.P. Root (Ed.), *Racially mixed people in America* (pp. 50-63). Newbury Park, CA: Sage.

Stephan, C. W., & Stephan, W. G. (1989). After intermarriage: Ethnic identity among mixed-heritage Japanese-Americans and Hispanics. *Journal of Marriage and the Family, 51,* 507-519.

Stephan, W. G., & Stephan, C. W. (1991). Intermarriage: Effects on personality, adjustment, and intergroup relations in two samples of students. *Journal of Marriage and Family, 53,* 241-250.

Sue, D. W., Arredondo, P., & McDavis, R. J. (1992). Multicultural counseling competencies and standards: A call to the profession. *Journal of Multicultural Counseling and Development, 20,* 64-88.

Sue, D. W., Carter, R. J., Casan, J. M., Fouad, N. A., Ivey, A. E., Jensen, M., LaFromboise, T., Manese, J. E., Ponteratto, J. G., & Vazquez-Nutall, E. (1998, March). *Multicultural counseling competencies: Individual, professional, and organizational development.* Thousand Oaks, CA: Sage.

Sue, D. W., & Sue, D. (1990). *Counseling the culturally different: Theory and practice* (2nd ed.). New York: Wiley.

Sullivan, A. (1995). Policy issues in gay and lesbian adoption. *Adoption and Fostering, 19,* 21-25.

Tafoya, T. (1997). Native gay and lesbian issues: The two-spirited. In B. Greene (Ed.), *Ethnic and cultural diversity among lesbians and gay men* (pp. 1-10). Thousand Oaks, CA: Sage.

Tafoya, T., & Rowell, R. (1988). Counseling Native American lesbians and gays. In M. Shernoff and W. A. Scott (Eds.), *A sourcebook of lesbian/gay health care* (pp. 63-67). Washington, DC: National Lesbian and Gay Health Foundation.

Tan, A. (1989). *The joy luck club.* New York: Putnam.

Taylor, R. J., & Thornton, M. C. (1996). Child welfare and transracial adoption. *Journal of Black Psychology, 22,* 282-291.

Thernstrom, S. (Ed). (1980). *Harvard encyclopedia of American ethnic groups.* Cambridge, MA: Belknap Press of Harvard University.

Thornton, M. C. (1983). *A social history of a multiethnic identity: The case of Black Japanese Americans.* Unpublished doctoral dissertation, University of Michigan, Ann Arbor.

Thornton, M. C. (1992). The quiet immigration: Foreign spouses of U. S. citizens, 1945-1985. In M.P.P. Root (Ed.), *Racially mixed people in America* (pp. 64-76). Newbury Park, CA: Sage.

Thornton, M. C. (1996). Hidden agendas, identity theories, and multiracial people. In M.P.P. Root (Ed.), *The multiracial experience: Racial boders as the new frontier* (pp. 101-120). Newbury Park, CA: Sage.

Thornton, M. C., & Wason, S. (1995). Intermarriage. In D. Levison (Ed.), *Encyclopedia of marriage and the family* (pp. 396-402). New York: Macmillan.

Tinker, J. N. (1982). Intermarriage and assimilations in a plural society: Japanese Americans in the United States. *Marriage and Family Review, 51*(1), 1-74.

Tizard, B., & Phoenix, A. (1995). The identity of mixed parentage adolescents. *Journal of Child Psychology and Psychiatry and Allied Disciplines, 36,* 1399-1410.

Trolley, B. C., Wallin, J., & Hansen, J. (1995). International adoption: Issues of acknowledgement of adoption and birth culture. *Child and Adolescent Social Work Journal, 12,* 465-479.

Tucker, L. (1996). Happy to be: Raising happy, healthy multiracial children in a racially divided society. *Interrace, 7*(1), 14-17.

Tucker, M., & Mitchell-Kernan, B. (1990). New trends in Black American interracial marriage: The social structural context. *Journal of Marriage and the Family, 52,* 209-218.

Turner, S., & Taylor, J. (1996). Unexplored issues in transracial adoption. *Journal of Black Psychology, 22,* 262-265.

U.S. Bureau of the Census. (1990). *Census of population: General population characteristics—United States* (Vol. 1990 CP-1-1). Washington, DC: Government Printing Office.

U.S. Bureau of the Census. (1998). *Statistical abstract of the United States: 1998* (118th ed.). Washington, DC: Author.

United States v. William S. Rogers, 11 U.S.C.S. 1105 (1846).

Valentine, G. (1995). Shades of gray: The conundrum of color categories. *Teaching Tolerance, 4*(1), 47.

von Sternberg, B. (1995a, April 12). "Biracial" doesn't mean one or the other. *Star Tribune,* pp. 1, 10A.

von Sternberg, B. (1995b, April 12). Redefining the races. Census categories are likely to change. *Star Tribune,* pp. 1, 10A.

Waldman, S., & Caplan, L. (1994, March 21). The politics of adoption. *Newsweek,* pp. 64-65.

Wardle, F. (1987). Are you sensitive to interracial children's special identity needs? *Young Children, 42*(2), 53-59.

Wardle, F. (1990). Who has ten fingers and light brown skin and likes to sing "Bingo?" Identity development of biracial children. *Dimensions, 18*(4), 24-25, 31.

Wardle, F. (1991). Interracial children and their families: How school social workers should respond. *Social Work in Education, 13,* 215-223.

Wardle, F. (1992a). Supporting biracial children in the school setting. *Education and Treatment of Children, 15,* 163-172.

Wardle, F. (1992b, March/April). Transracial and interracial adoption: The myth of cultural genocide. *Interrace,* 29-31.

Wardle, F. (1993, April). Interracial families and biracial children. *Child Care Information Exchange,* pp. 45-48.

Wardle, F., & Baptiste, D. A. (1988). Growing up biracially in America: The inalienable rights of biracial children. *Nurturing Today, 9*(4), 9, 21.

Wehrly, B. (1995). *Pathways to multicultural counseling competence: A developmental journey.* Belmont, CA: Wadsworth.

Wehrly, B. (1996). *Counseling interracial individuals and families.* Alexandria, VA: American Counseling Association.

Wehrly, B. (1998). Bibliotherapy. In H. G. Rosenthal (Ed.), *Favorite counseling and therapy techniques: 51 therapists share their most creative strategies* (pp. 185-188). Bristol, PA: Accelerated Development.

Wiggins, C. (1998, May 3). Anomalous like me. *Washington Post,* p. F8.

Wilkinson, H. S. (1995). Psycholegal process and issues in international adoption. *American Journal of Family Therapy, 23,* 173-183.

Willhoite, M. (1990). *Daddy's roommate.* Boston: Alyson.

Williams, G. H. (1995). *Life on the color line: The true story of a White boy who discovered he was Black.* New York: Dutton.

Williams, T. K. (1992). Prism lives: Identity of binational Amerasians. In M.P.P. Root (Ed.), *Racially mixed people in America* (pp. 280-303). Newbury Park, CA: Sage.

Williams, T. K. (1996). Race as process: Reassessing the "What are you?" encounters of biracial individuals. In M.P.P. Root (Ed.), *The multiracial experience: Racial borders as the new frontier* (pp. 191-210). Newbury Park, CA: Sage.

Williams, T. K. (1997). Race-ing and being raced: The critical interrogation of "passing." *Amerasia Journal, 23*(1), 61-65.

Williamson, J. (1980). *New people: Miscegenation and mulattoes in the United States.* New York: Free Press.

Willis, M. G. (1996). The real issues in transracial adoption: A response. *Journal of Black Psychology, 22,* 246-253.

Wilson, T. P. (1992). Blood quantum: Native American mixed bloods. In M.P.P. Root (Ed.), *Racially mixed people in America* (pp. 108-125). Newbury Park, CA: Sage.

Winik, L. W. (1998, August 2). It's about love. *Parade Magazine,* pp. 4-7.

Winn, N. N., & Priest, R. (1993). Counseling biracial children: A forgotten component of multicultural counseling. *Family Therapy, 20,* 29-36.

Wolfman, I. (1991). *Do people grow on family trees? Genealogy for kids & other beginners.* New York: Workman.

Wong, M. G. (1989). A look at intermarriage among the Chinese in the United States in 1980. *Sociological Perspectives, 32*(1), 87-107.

Yasinski, J. (1998). Fact vs. fiction. *Interrace, 8*(2), 8.

Author Index

177

Subject Index

About the Authors

Bea Wehrly, Ph.D., N.C.C., has 40 years of experience in teaching and counseling, the last 25 of which were at Western Illinois University. She is the author of *Pathways to Multicultural Counseling Competence: A Developmental Journey* (1995) and *Counseling Interracial Individuals and Families* (1996). She developed and taught the multicultural counseling course at Western Illinois University for the 8 years before she retired. Most recently, she has been conducting seminars on multiracial counseling in the United States, Canada, and Europe. She is the 1999 recipient of the ACA Professional Development award.

Kelley R. Kenney, Ed.D., is Full Professor and Counselor at Kutztown University of Pennsylvania and Adjunct Professor at Chestnut Hill College of Philadelphia. She has over 15 years of counseling, supervision, teaching, and consultation experience. Her areas of interest and specialization include college student development, sexuality and HIV/AIDS awareness, diversity and multicultural issues, and multiracial individuals and families. She has presented programs, conducted workshops, and published on a number of these issues for local, regional, national, and international conferences and meetings. She will serve as Chair of the North Atlantic Region American Counseling Association for 2000-2001.

Mark E. Kenney, M.Ed., N.C.C., is a counselor at Albright College in Reading, PA. His professional experince includes teaching in special education, secondary education, and higher education settings. As a counselor, he has worked in both private practice and college settings. His areas of specialization include academic intervention and mediation, adolescent male identity development, gay and lesbian issues, children coping with divorce, and fathering issues. He is a certified diversity trainer for the National Coalition Building Institute, as well as a certified presenter for the STEP Parenting program. He has done a significant amount of research on the historical context of interracial marriage and multiracialism and has been called upon as a consultant and presenter on these topics. He is the husband of Dr. Kelley Kenney.

Please remember that this is a library book,
and that it belongs only temporarily to each
person who uses it. Be considerate. Do
not write in this, or any, library book.

DATE DUE

JE 04 '01			
12/22/01			
AUG 2 3 2002			
AP 16 '06			
JE 0 '06			
GAYLORD			PRINTED IN U.S.A.